Physical Characteristics of the Pointer

(from The Kennel (

D1080459

Colour: Usual colours are lemon and white, orange and white, liver and white, and black and white. Self colours and tricolours are also correct.

Body: Well sprung ribs carried well back gradually falling away at strong muscular and slightly arched loins. Short-coupled. Haunch bones well spaced and prominent, not above level of back.

Tail: Medium length, thick at root, tapering gradually to a point. Well covered with close hair, carried on a level with back, with no upward curl. In movement, tail should lash from side to side.

Hindquarters: Very muscular. Well turned stifles. Good expanse of first and second thigh. Hocks well let down.

Coat: Fine, short, hard and evenly distributed, perfectly smooth and straight with decided sheen.

Size: Desirable heights at withers: dogs: 63–69 cms (25–27 ins); bitches: 61–66 cms (24–26 ins).

Feet: Oval, well knit, arched toes, well cushioned.

Pointer

◇

by Richard G Beauchamp

Profit through Skill

Moulton
College
NORTHAMPTONSHIRE

Table of Contents

9

History of the Pointer

Deriving from the swift-moving hunters and scenting gun dogs, the Pointer represents England's quintessential pointing dog. Meet the Pointer and its predecessors from the Continent and contributing breeds, whose combination yielded this 'paragon of the pointing breeds.'

24

Characteristics of the Pointer

Take home the strikingly beautiful and athletic Pointer, but first be aware of the breed's needs and personality traits. New owners must be willing to accept the responsibilities of handling such an active, intelligent breed and learn how to stay 'one step ahead' of the swift, high-energy Pointer.

36

Breed Standard for the Pointer

Learn the requirements of a well-bred Pointer by studying the description of the breed set forth in The Kennel Club standard. Both show dogs and pets must possess key characteristics as outlined in the breed standard.

42

Your Puppy Pointer

Be advised about choosing a reputable breeder and selecting a healthy, typical puppy. Understand the responsibilities of ownership, including home preparation, acclimatisation, the vet and prevention of common puppy problems.

PUBLISHED IN THE
UNITED KINGDOM BY:

INTERPET
PUBLISHING

Vincent Lane, Dorking
Surrey RH4 3YX
England

ISBN 1-903098-55-6

70

Everyday Care of Your Pointer

Enter into a sensible discussion of dietary and feeding considerations, exercise, grooming, travelling and identification of your dog. This chapter discusses Pointer care for all stages of development.

90

Housebreaking and Training Your Pointer

by Charlotte Schwartz
Be informed about the importance of training your Pointer from the basics of housebreaking and understanding the development of a young dog to executing obedience commands (sit, stay, down, etc.).

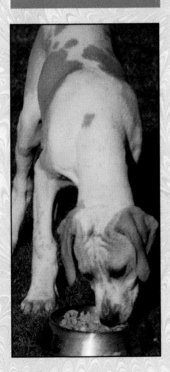

PHOTOS BY CAROL ANN JOHNSON AND MICHAEL TRAFFORD, WITH ADDITIONAL PHOTOS BY:

Erica and John Bandes
James Basham
Norvia Behling
TJ Calhoun
Carolina Biological Supply
Doskocil
Isabelle Francais
James Hayden-Yoav
James R Hayden, RBP

Bill Jonas
Alice van Kempen
Dwight R Kuhn
Dr Dennis Kunkel
Mikki Pet Products
Phototake
Jean Claude Revy
Dr Andrew Spielman
C James Webb

Illustrations by Renée Low

146

Showing Your Pointer

Experience the dog show world, including different types of shows and the making up of a champion. Go beyond the conformation ring to working trials and agility trials, etc.

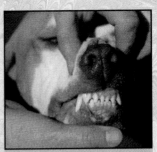

115

Health Care of Your Pointer

Discover how to select a proper veterinary surgeon and care for your dog at all stages of life. Topics include vaccination scheduling, skin problems, dealing with external and internal parasites and the medical and behavioural conditions common to the breed.

Special thanks to Erica and John Bandes, Barbara Cherry, Wendy Gordon and the rest of the owners of dogs featured in this book.

Countries throughout Europe have developed their own versions of 'pointing dogs,' but the breed that bears the name Pointer is the one hailing from England, shown here.

History of the
POINTER

In *The Natural History of Dogs*, a fascinating and enlightening study of the development of the dog breeds of the world, authors Richard and Alice Feinnes classify most dogs as having descended from one of four major groups, all which trace back to separate and distinct branches of the wolf family. These four classifications are the Dingo Group, the Greyhound Group, the Northern Group and the Mastiff Group. It is important to have at least a basic understanding of these groups as very few breeds of dog are of pure descent; instead, they owe their widely diverse characteristics to an intermingling of the blood of as many as all four of the groups.

The Dingo Group traces its origin to the Asian wolf (*Canis lupus pallipes*). Two well-known examples of the Dingo Group are the Basenji and, through the admixture of several European breeds, the Rhodesian Ridgeback.

The Greyhound Group descends from a coursing-type relative of the Asian wolf. The group includes all those dogs that hunt by sight and are capable of great speed. The Greyhound itself, the Afghan Hound, the Borzoi and

Braque d'Auvergne, one of the many pointers of France, stands 24 inches high and is marked in a black and white roaning pattern.

The Italian Pointer is known as the Bracco Italiano, coloured in chestnut, orange, and/or white. Beyond Italy, it has a small following in Britain.

Braque du Bourbonnais, roaned in brown, liver or orange, is also known as the Bourbonnais Pointer, another French hunting dog.

the Irish Wolfhound are all examples of this group. These dogs also are known as the coursing breeds or sighthounds, though they are not true hounds as they do not hunt by scent. It is worth noting that the Pointer has been influenced by this group of swift-moving hunters.

The Arctic or Nordic Group of dogs is a direct descendant of the rugged Northern wolf (*Canis lupus*). Included in this group are the Alaskan Malamute, Chow Chow, German Shepherd, and the much smaller Pointer and Spitz-type dog.

The fourth classification, and the one that is of special interest to those who wish to research the history of the Pointer, is the Mastiff Group. This group owes its primary heritage to the Tibetan wolf (*Canis lupus chanco* or *laniger*). The great diversity of dogs included in this group indicates that they are not entirely of pure blood as they have undoubtedly been influenced by descendants of the other three groups.

The widely divergent descendants of the Mastiff Group are known to include many of the scenting breeds—breeds that find game by the use of their olfactory senses rather than by sight. These breeds include those we now classify as gun dogs and the true hounds.

As man became more sophisticated and his lifestyle more complex, he found that he could produce dogs that could suit his specific needs from these descendants of the wolf. Often these needs were based upon the manner in which man himself went after game on particular terrain. The importance here is that man had taken control of the individual dogs that mated. Specific characteristics were prized and inbreeding practices were employed to perpetuate these characteristics.

One type of hunting dog that man developed retained the wolf characteristics of pursuing the prey until it was cornered and killed or chased up a tree. This practice is more or less typical of that group of dogs known today as our scenthounds. While their tenacity was held in high regard, a hound's willingness to continue the chase for miles, if necessary, often became rather tiresome for their owners. Thus was born a need for the hunting dog that never followed through with the chase or the attack. The dog's job was not to do the hunting or killing, but rather to assist the human hunter by finding the game and indicating its discovery to the hunter quietly so as not to scare away the birds. Furthermore, like any good assistant, the dog obeyed its master's commands without hesitation.

References have been made to

Perdiguero de Burgos is one of the largest hunting dogs, standing up to 30 inches and weighing 66 pounds. He is known as the Spanish Pointer and is a gifted multi-tasked hunting dog.

A well-balanced pointing dog, the Braque St. Germain derived from the Pointer and is characteristically coloured in orange and white.

German Shorthaired Pointer is one of the popular pointing breeds from Germany, known for his working excellence and his liver coloration.

The prototypical Greyhound has been used to add speed, elegance and stamina to many breeds.

Adding tenacity, strength and white coloration, the Bull Terrier is mentioned in the creation of many breeds of dog.

The Pointer, whose ancestors are many and greatly varied, today possesses a purity and nobility that is all his own.

the existence of this kind of dog as early as the time of the ancient Greeks. Written records point to the existence of a rough-coated breed of dog in Italy that signalled its discovery of game to the hunter by assuming a rigid position and placing its body in direct line with the find.

Today we think of the Pointer as a distinct breed of dog but in fact the name refers to a dog that works the field in a distinctive manner, not unlike that described in ancient Greece. Countries throughout Europe developed their own unique breed of 'pointer' or 'pointing dog' based upon the demands made by their specific terrain. The results of these efforts can be seen in Italy's Bracco Italiano and Italian Spinone, Germany's Shorthaired and Wirehaired Pointers, the Braque Francais and Brittany of France, as well as Britain's contribution, the breed known simply as the Pointer.

Popular but controversial opinion has influenced many to believe that all of the pointing breeds owe their basic foundation to Spain and that the Pointer, as developed in Great Britain, owes its source exclusively to the Spanish Pointer, the *Perdiguero de Burgos*. However, a good many of the aficionados of Britain's Pointer beg to differ.

The Pointer and His Predecessors, written by William

Arkwright of Sutton Scarsdale, near Chesterfield, is the most universally accepted work on the development of the Pointer breed. He began work on his book late in the 19th century and researched the material included over a period of 30 years. Throughout this work, Arkwright, while fully admitting the existence of a Spanish Pointer in England,

German Wirehaired Pointer, known in the Fatherland as the Deutscher Drahthaariger Vorstehhund, is a highly resourceful hunting dog, popular around the world.

The Foxhound represents the classic scenthound of Britain and has been used in the 'perfecting' of many breeds.

POINTERS ON THE CONTINENT

Every major European nation has produced its own version of the Pointer, with Germany and France leading the list. France has nine such breeds, including the multi-talented Brittany, Wirehaired Pointing Griffon, also called Korthals Griffon, and the seven Braques named for their regions, such as the Auvergne, Bourbonnais and Saint-Germain. Germany has six distinct pointing breeds, including the Stichelhaar, Weimaraner, Pudelpointer and the German Short-, Wire- and Longhaired Pointers.

Hungary boasts its talented Vizsla; Slovakia its Cesky Fousek; the Slavs, their incredibly popular Dalmatian; Italy its Bracco Italiano and Segugio Italiano, both gaining fans in the UK; Spain its Perdiguero de Burgos and Navarro; and Portugal its Perdigueiro Portugueso. Belgium's Shorthaired Pointer is considered extremely rare, as are the two Danish breeds, the Old Danish Bird Dog (or *Gammel Dansk Hønsehund*) and the Hertha Pointer.

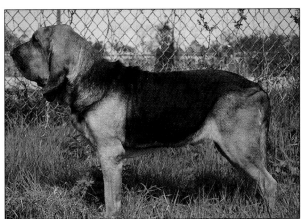

Few breeds can compete with the Bloodhound for reliability of nose and determination— desirable qualities in all hunting dogs.

maintained that the influence of the Spanish dog had little, if any, effect on the development of his chosen breed.

Lending credence to Arkwright's belief is *Anecdotes of Dogs*, written by Edward Jesse, Esq, and published in 1880. Jesse wrote of the Spanish Pointer in England during his day and describes a dog so unlike the Pointer as we know it that it is difficult to associate the two

fox-hound of that era had the conformation that would produce the lithe lines and increased speed of the Pointer as we know it. Arkwright not only dismisses the Spanish dog as the foundation of the Pointer, he also casts doubt on Spain as the origin of the pointing breeds in the first place. He refers to a letter written by the US Vice Consul in Valencia, Spain in 1900. In that letter the Vice Consul stated that pointing dogs

A photograph from the turn of the 20th century, showing trained Pointers in the field. The photo was captioned 'Waiting the Flight.'

breeds. 'How well do I recollect in my early youth seeing the slow, heavy, solemn-looking, and thick-shoulderd (*sic*) Spanish pointer, tired with two or three hours' work in turnips, and so stiff after it the next day, as to be little capable of resuming his labours.'

Although he does go on to explain away the streamlining of the breed by a simple cross to the 'fox-hound,' certainly one would question whether the so-called

existed in Spain for many genera-tions and were the descendants of an original pair that were presented as gifts to the Spanish Court 'by an Italian prince.'

Colonel David Hancock has researched this question of origin quite thoroughly in his excellent work *The Heritage of the Dog*, and the Drury book *British Dogs* revealed that the first record of the Pointer in Great Britain is the Tilleman painting of the Duke of

ADAPTABILITY & SOPHISTICATION

Hunting has demanded different skills through the ages and the dogs that man has used in this pursuit have also changed. In the earliest stages, man hunted to obtain food and to rid himself of dangerous beasts. As man developed his techniques, and hunting began to be regulated by the government, it became a sporting event and the duties of his dogs became increasingly complex. Those who fancy the Pointer as a hunter believe that their breed represents the highest level of canine adaptability and sophistication.

Kingston with his kennel of pointers in 1725. Drury describes these dogs as '...the same elegant Franco-Italian type as the pointing dogs painted by Oudry (1686–1755) and Desportes (1661–1743) at the end of the 17th century.'

Finally, and contrary to what has been readily accepted by many theorists, research indicates that the French pointer was well established in France long before the Spanish Pointer made its way to Great Britain. Moreover, those dogs, very frequently seen throughout Great Britain, far more closely resembled the Pointer of today than the Spanish dogs.

In 1895 this rare black bitch, Leader, made a name for herself in the field. She belonged to Mr W Arkwright.

Drayton Lady and Ch Coronation, a brace of show and working Pointer bitches owned by Mr H Sawtell. Circa 1935.

Above: Sandford Dum Dum is an example of an old-time Pointer, produced from Foxhound and Spanish Pointer breeding.

POINTER COLOUR
It is believed that the solid-coloured Pointers are the result of the cross that was made to the Greyhound many generations ago. On occasion, solid-colour black, liver and, more rarely, orange and lemon Pointers may be seen. The highly developed eyesight of the Pointer can easily be attributed to the breed's sighthound ancestor, as can a Pointer's aloof and aristo-cratic demeanour.

Ch Flagon of Ardagh was a top winner of the late 1920s/early 1930s. He added to his many honours two further Challenge Certificates in 1933, at the age of seven.

PERFORMING THE ENTIRE RANGE OF SKILLS

The Pointer owes a good deal of the respect it enjoys among hunters to the popularity of what was called 'wing-shooting' or shooting the game in air. To accomplish this, a dog had first to locate the birds by scent and then alert the hunter to their presence by standing at point. When the hunter approached, or upon signal, the dog would flush out the covey and set the birds to wing. Although many breeds were accomplished at perhaps one of these skills, few could compare to Britain's Pointer in the excellent manner in which they performed the entire range.

OTHER INFLUENCES

'Horses for courses' is an old saying among British stockmen that has served as the basis for the development of many kinds of prized livestock. Translated in layman's terms, this adage simply refers to choosing a breeding formula that will produce a horse best suited to work in the terrain of the region. This formula not only applied to horses but also was the basis upon which many of Britain's outstanding dog breeds were developed. Often this practice required going to totally unrelated breeds for what was needed. At times a dash of one breed, a smattering of another and perhaps even a sprinkling of two of three others were necessary to complete the recipe for the ideal dog! Although this practice was not particularly something to be

This original painting of a Spanish Pointer by renowned dog artist Reinagle appeared in *The Sportsman's Cabinet* in 1803.

This photo, circa 1930, was captioned 'Pointers at School on the Moors.'

Nancolleth Billy Mischief was the name of this dog bred by Mrs F A Rowe in 1931.

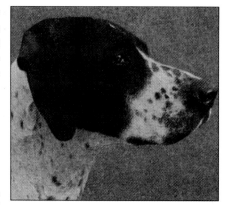

TROPHY MODEL

One of the legendary show Pointers of all time was Ch Lune Prince, owned by Mr T Moorby. Prince was so revered by enthusiasts of the breed that he was used as a model by the Pointer Club for one of its trophies. During his career in the ring, he obtained 700 firsts and 33 Challenge Certificates.

Rock of Ballymoy, a Pointer of the 1930s, was bred by Mr G Davies and owned by Mrs M V Christian.

REMARKABLE!

One of the most remarkable Pointers in the breed's history was the dog Drake, who had been bred by Sir R Garth and sold by him at what was then considered a 'staggering figure' to Mr R J Lloyd Price of Wales. The dog was then at the advanced age of seven years but was said to work the field far better than even puppies of the highest class. The speed at which he worked was such that he sent up a cloud of dust when he stopped to drop to the scent of game.

His Grace the Duke of Montrose was a renowned Pointer expert who owned one of the most important kennels of the breed. Two Pointers of his breeding are shown (foreground) in this photo taken at the 1930 Ulster Gun Trials.

shouted from the housetops, it is to what we owe the incredible characteristics of some of our modern-day breeds, including the Pointer.

Perhaps the question of the Pointer's country of origin will never be satisfactorily answered, but there is no doubt that the gene pool of its descendants is certainly diverse. Breed historians acknowledge that at least four crosses to other breeds were employed to bring about the Pointer as we know it today. The four breeds credited are the Greyhound, the Bloodhound, the Foxhound and, more surprisingly, the Bull Terrier.

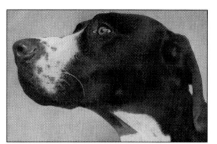

Nancolleth Remarkable, a liver-and-white Pointer bred and owned by Mrs A Rowe, was a Crufts winner in 1932.

DOG SHOW CONQUERED
England's prestigious Crufts Dog Show has been conquered by the Pointer on two occasions, the first of which was in 1935 by Pennine Prima Donna, owned by A Eggleston, and the second in 1958 by Ch Chiming Bells, owned by Mrs W Parkinson.

Jake's Carolina Boy, an American-bred Pointer of the 1930s. He was owned by Miss Claudia Lea Phelps and won the Amateur Derby Stakes, held by the Pinehurst Field Trials Club in Pinehurst, North Carolina, USA.

At first reading, these crosses may seem to be somewhat bizarre choices. However, you will see how these crosses made perfect sense in our forefathers' attempt to produce the ideal hunting dog. You will also see that these astute breeders had to take a bit of the bitter for the sake of the sweet. There are a number of problems resulting from these crosses that continue to haunt the breed today, hundreds of generations later.

Let us look first at the Greyhound cross. There can be no doubt that the use of Greyhound blood gave the modern Pointer its speed, elegance and grace. The short sleek coat hearkens back to the breed's Greyhound ancestor as does the long, well-arched neck, graceful underline and turn-on-the-spot agility. On the other hand, the Greyhound cross can plague the breeder with excessive refinement of head. A narrow front and rib cage, a tilted pelvis and excessive loin arch are also undesirable characteristics that sometimes appear in the Pointer.

The Pointer is not alone in its use of the ancient Bloodhound for its highly developed scenting ability and robust constitution. The undesirable features that accompanied those highly desirable Bloodhound characteristics, however, were the plodding movement, long rounded ears and straight underline, with which Pointer breeders are still forced to contend.

Foxhound blood was also incorporated for scenting ability and easy maintenance. The well-developed rib cage and relentless endurance were positive assets as well. Such advantages were not without their price, however, as round bone, plain heads, long ropy tails carried vertically and houndy underlines plague the breed to this day.

There are probably few breeds any more alert or persistent and determined than the Bull Terrier, and this is what the early Pointer breeders sought. However, the barrel chest, the overly broad front and the hard-bitten terrier eye and expression were contributions the Pointer did not need.

Despite such problems, the Pointer breed rapidly took shape

and the future of the breed was certainly given a major boost in the right direction by the aristocratic names who took up the breed: Lord Lichfield, the Duke of Kingston, Lord Mexborough and the Earl of Lauderdale, just to name a few.

Four early dogs are generally given credit for laying the foundation for all that was to come in the breed: Brocton's Bounce, Stater's Major, Whitehouse's Hamlet and Garth's Drake (who was said to be one-eighth Foxhound) were the names that dominated Pointer circles. Ch Ranger, a dog owned by Mr Newton, became the breed's first bench champion, winning three first prizes at England's premier events—Leeds and Birmingham in 1861, and the final award at Chelsea in 1863. Ch Flash gained her title at Birmingham in 1865. The first

Mrs Parker arrives at the 1934 Crufts Dog Show with four of Mrs N Holt's Pointers, having travelled from North Wales.

field trial champion was Drake, born in 1868, bred and owned by Sir Richard Garth. Henry Sawtell

A Pointer bitch bred in Italy, working the mountains of her native country.

Stainton Startler was born in 1932 and won his first Challenge Certificate in 1933 at the Scottish Kennel Club Show.

Pennine Prima Donna, born in 1931, is not considered a Champion despite winning 12 Challenge Certificates in conformation shows. No gundog can become a Champion without also earning a Field Trial Certificate, which this Pointer did not do.

Of crucial importance was his unmatched ability to perform in the field. Here was a tenacious hunter willing to meet the demands of any job assigned to him. Descriptions such as 'a paragon of the pointing breeds,' and 'a non-stop hunting machine' reverberated throughout the hillsides, sounding loud and clear across the Channel to the Continent and then across the Atlantic to America.

It is in America, in particular, that Britain's classic hunter was welcomed with open arms, not just by hunters but by show enthusiasts as well. While field Pointers greatly outnumber show Pointers in the US, the breed still does nicely in the show ring. The Pointer became the symbol of the nation's most prestigious dog show, the Westminster Kennel Club show, and took the honour of Best in Show at that show three times during the 20th century. The first Pointer to win Westminster was R F Maloney's Ch Governor Moscow in 1925. The second of these victories was claimed by Ch Nancolleth Markable, owned by the famous Giralda Farms, in 1932. Over 50 years later, in 1986, Ch Marjetta's National Acclaim, owned by Mrs A R Robson and Michael Zollo, won Best in Show at Madison Square Garden in New York City, the third and last Pointer to win Westminster in the century.

bred and owned the breed's first dual champion, Faskally Brag, who was also a sire of significant impact.

In the end, British stockmanship produced an elegant animal, strikingly painted, blessed with exquisite balance and proportion.

Pointers are seen in several colours and, while marking patterns may appear similar and recognisable, each Pointer's markings are unique.

Characteristics of the
POINTER

Some remarkable characteristics of the Pointer are the breed's exceptionally high energy level, directness of purpose and zest for life. However, there are also the more subtle and telling things that make the Pointer the unique breed that it is. Living with the breed reveals both the Pointer's innate intelligence and uncanny ability to work things out.

The average Pointer doesn't 'need' people; he accepts them. If it were possible to ask your Pointer if he required some assistance, the answer might well be, 'I can manage that by myself very well, thank you.' A Pointer might well think this is so; however, a Pointer must have direction and discipline. You must never forget, this is a dog carefully bred through history for speed, stamina and intelligence—admirable but lethal qualities if not properly channelled.

The Pointer's striking appearance has, in many cases, been the reason for selecting the breed as a household pet. Unfortunately, too often the needs of the breed are ignored. The person owning a Pointer must respond to this highly intelligent breed's athleticism.

If the owner of a Pointer cannot guarantee his dog at least one hour of daily exercise, then there must be someone in the household who can. Then and only then can the Pointer become the ideal family dog. Otherwise, the potential owner should consider a different, less active breed.

If such care and training can be provided, it is still important not to act hastily. For the Pointer who is destined to be an all-round family and house dog, it is better to choose from a breeder who has selected for characteristics that include an eye to the show ring and companionship rather than from a breeder who is concentrating exclusively on hunting. Hunting dogs may be far too active for the average family, though it is also necessary to screen show breeders carefully as well.

People are attracted to the Pointer for many reasons: its

beauty and deportment are legendary. Other owners wax lyrical about the intelligence and ability of Pointers in the field and even in day-to-day life. Besides these attributes, there is a wide range of beautiful colours and markings from which to choose.

However, all of these characteristics do not constitute reason enough for anyone to purchase a Pointer without the prospective owner conducting a little self-evaluation as well.

This is not a breed that can be left home alone all day long and then be taken out for a five-minute walk in the evening.

Hundreds of generations of selective breeding make the Pointer a dog that must run. The breed, no matter from what lines it may come, has the innate desire to experience the great outdoors and perform its duties as a hunter of game.

A Pointer can be a great companion and close friend for its entire lifespan but only if the owner is ready to invest the time, patience and exercise outdoors required to bring the breed to its full potential.

Pointer pups are very cute. Their floppy ears, elastic physiques and waggy-tail personalities make them well nigh

The Pointer is a very active dog that requires as much exercise as possible; an hour each day is the absolute minimum.

MENTAL AND PHYSICAL

Everything in the Pointer's history contributed to the mental and physical characteristics that have produced both an industrious, efficient hunting dog and a fine household companion. Generations of selection on that basis give us dogs that are happiest when they can please their owner.

investigating, digging, chewing, eating, relieving itself and needing to go outdoors, only to immediately insist that it be let back in. Any prospective owner should also remember that puppies experience just as many of the aches and pains and sniffles as any human child on the way to maturity.

It takes time and planning to fulfil the day-to-day needs of a puppy or grown dog. This says nothing of the time required for the many lessons a Pointer must be taught by its master before it understands what it may and may not do.

Some breeds live simply to please their masters in that they always seem ready, willing and able to respond to commands. The Pointer, however, has to know that you are serious about what you ask it to do, and it may have to think about it as well. What is vital to remember is that your Pointer puppy, or even adult, will depend wholly upon you for everything it needs and every lesson it must learn. If you are not ready to accept that responsibility, you are not ready to own a Pointer. It will only result in household damage and drudgery on your part, and what should be a joyful relationship will result in a frustrating situation for both you and your dog.

irresistible. Indeed, Pointer puppies are the subject of calendars and greeting cards printed around the world each year. It is important to realise, however, that a Pointer puppy will spend only a very small part of its day sitting and looking cute. The far greater part of the day will be spent

Failure to understand the amount of time and consideration a well-cared-for dog requires is one of the primary reasons for the number of unwanted canines that end their lives in an animal shelter. Given proper consideration beforehand, the purchase of a dog can bring many years of companionship and comfort as well as unconditional love and devotion no other animal can match.

Before any family brings a dog into their home they should give very serious consideration to three extremely important questions:

1. *Does the person who will ultimately be responsible for the dog's day-to-day care really want a dog?*

The children in the family may vociferously claim that they desperately want a dog; however, will they be doing more than just playing with the dog once it arrives? Pet care can be an excellent way to teach children responsibility, but it should not be forgotten that in their enthusiasm to have a puppy, children are apt to promise almost anything. It is what will happen after the novelty of owning a new dog has worn off that must be considered.

In many active families the ultimate responsibility for the family dog often falls on one person. This appears to be the

The Pointer is as well known for his good looks and striking markings as he is for his skill in the field.

case even in the homes where both parents work outside the home. This person may not relish any more duties than he or she already has!

2. *Does the lifestyle and schedule of the household lend itself to the demands of proper dog care?*

There must always be someone available to see to a dog's basic needs: feeding,

27

THE DEVOTED 'NANNY'
One of the Pointer's most striking characteristics is the kind and gentle manner with which it conducts itself in the company of children. Even the most accomplished field dog has a very special place reserved for youngsters. Many owners state that the speed demon at work in the field can become quite the devoted 'nanny' in dealing with the family's children. The Pointer raised with children is as much their protector as their playmate.

exercise, training and so on. If you or your family are gone from morning to night or if you travel frequently and are away from home for long periods of time, the dog must still be cared for. A Pointer cannot be left home alone, day in and day out. Are you willing and able to adjust your schedule or are you prepared to pay the costs of frequent boarding kennels for your dog while you are gone?

3. *Is this particular breed, the Pointer, suitable for the individual or household?*

Does your household contain children? Pointers are wonderful with well-behaved children and they make delightful playmates, but no dog should be expected to tolerate abuse just because a child knows no better. At the same time, an enthusiastic Pointer puppy can knock down and injure a toddler in a playful moment.

The prospective dog owner should also strongly consider the specific peculiarities of his own lifestyle and household. Everyone involved must realise that the new dog will not understand the household routine and must be taught everything you want it to know and do. This takes time and patience, and often the most important lessons for the new dog to learn will take the longest for it to absorb.

WHY A PUREBRED?
There is no difference in the love, devotion and companion-ship that a mixed-breed dog and a purebred dog can give its owner. There are, however, some aspects that can best be fulfilled by the purebred dog.

Not all puppies will grow up to be particularly attractive adults or they may appeal only to someone with very exotic tastes. If you have a specific image in mind of what your dream dog looks like, you are best not taking the chance with a mongrel. For instance, the haystack look of the Old English Sheepdog would not be suitable for someone who thinks the razor-sharp lines of the Dobermann are what the perfect dog should have. Predicting what a mixed-breed puppy will look like at maturity is well nigh impossible. Size, length of hair and temperament can change drastically between puppyhood and adulthood and may not be at all what the owner had hoped for. Then what happens to the dog?

In buying a well-bred Pointer puppy, the purchaser will have a very good idea of what the dog will look like at maturity as well as how it will be capable of behaving with proper guidance. If your mental picture of the ideal dog is a Cocker Spaniel or an English Setter that lives only to lavish attention and affection upon you, the more independent breeds (of which the Pointer is certainly one) are not going to live up to that ideal. Naturally

Pointers are playful dogs who make fun companions. Here's a surfing pup 'riding the waves' with a little help from his family.

there are differences within breeds just as there are differences from family to family and from human to human. At the same time, the general character of a specific breed is far more predictable than that of a dog of unknown parentage.

When choosing a puppy, one must have the adult dog in mind because the little fellow is going to be an adult much longer than it ever was a puppy. The adult dog is what must fit the owner's lifestyle and aesthetic standards.

A fastidious housekeeper may well have second thoughts when trying to accommodate a very large breed that slobbers or one that casts its coat all year 'round. All dogs cast coat to some degree. Pointer hair is shorter and less noticeable on clothing and furniture but far more difficult than long hair to pick up with a Hoover or a brush.

The initial purchase price of a Pointer could easily be a significant investment for the owner, but a purebred dog costs no more to maintain than a mixed breed, unless of course it is blest with the coat of a Maltese or Poodle, which the Pointer is not. If the cost of having exactly the kind of dog you want and are proud to own is amortised over the number of years you will enjoy it, you must admit the initial cost becomes far less consequential.

WHO SHOULD OWN A POINTER?

Just as a prospective buyer should have a checklist to lead him or her to a responsible breeder so must good breeders have a list of qualifications for the buyer. These are just a few of the 'musts' a prospective Pointer buyer might face if looking to purchase a puppy from a responsible breeder:

1. The buyer must have a fenced garden and a secure and protected place for the dog to stay if the owner is away.
2. Children should be at least five years of age. Although Pointers seem to have a natural affinity for children, an adolescent Pointer can be clumsy and can unintentionally injure a toddler.
3. Pointers are usually too strong and active for elderly people.
4. Everyone in the family must want a Pointer.
5. The buyer must be able financially to provide proper veterinary and home care.
6. No Pointer is likely to be sold to parties who are interested in breeding 'just pets' or operating an indiscriminate 'stud factory.'
7. The buyer must be aware that Pointers require a great deal of exercise.

THE POINTER AS A HOUSE DOG

A young Pointer must start understanding household rules from the moment it enters your home. What it will take to accomplish this is patience, love and a firm but gentle and unrelenting hand. Even the youngest Pointer puppy understands the difference between being corrected and being abused.

Pointers are entirely capable of being anyone's best friend and household companion but, as is the case in any good relationship, both parties must be compatible. Pointers were bred to hunt. At no time in the breed's developmental history was any attempt made to make the Pointer a lap dog or boudoir companion. A Pointer best belongs to someone who realises that work can come in the form of almost any structured activity—performing the daily obedience routine or even playing ball.

Pointers must be given their daily duties and opportunities to exercise or they may well use up their excess time by inventing things to do. What your Pointer decides to do on its own might be gnawing the legs of your best table, digging a tunnel to the neighbour's garden or communicating vocally with every other canine in the hemisphere. As far as your Pointer is concerned, if

ONE STEP AHEAD

An excellent example of the Pointer's speed and endurance comes from the field. It is said that the reason the Pointer is so successful in the field is that it covers so much ground in the course of a hunt. Many estimate that covering 100 miles in a full day's hunt is not unusual for a big running Pointer. This, combined with the breed's often unbridled enthusiasm for its work, can result in the dog's becoming quite out of control. None of these characteristics disappears because a Pointer has been chosen as a house dog and companion. Therefore, the owner of a companion Pointer must always be one step ahead of his dog and always in control.

A bored Pointer is a Pointer who will find something to do to entertain himself. Avoid destructive behaviour by providing ample exercise and involving the dog in the family's activities.

you do not insist that something it is doing must be stopped, your lack of determination will be construed as *carte blanche* or freedom to continue! Pointers learn quickly, but that does not mean they always care about what you are trying to impress upon them! Moreover, if you do not provide the requisite leadership, your Pointer will let you know in no uncertain terms that it is entirely capable of providing that leadership for itself.

The Pointer is short of coat and long on endurance, particularly tolerant of heat and, considering the breed's thin single coat, fairly tolerant of the cold as well. However, the Pointer must still be left in the shade when temperatures soar or housed indoors when they plummet.

The Pointer is curious and will want to roam if not provided with a fenced garden. The Pointer can be trained to do just about anything a dog is capable of doing, particularly if the task includes agility and enthusiasm.

MALE OR FEMALE?
While some people may have personal preferences as to the sex of their dog, both the male and the female Pointer make equally good companions and are equal in their trainability. The decision will have more to do with the lifestyle and ultimate plans of the owner than with differences between the sexes in the breed.

Pointers from lines bred strictly for the field are usually smaller and finer boned. They also seem to pack more energy ounce for ounce in their physiques.

Pointers from show stock lines are generally larger and have heavier bone than their field cousins. The male is normally larger and heavier boned than the female at maturity.

Males usually take a longer time to grow up both mentally and physically. Some males can reach a point during adolescence when they could not care less about food, and keeping the young male in reasonable weight may prove to be somewhat of a challenge. This is not to say that young Pointer females are exempt from these disturbing hunger strikes, but experience has proven that males are apt to take the lead here.

The female is not entirely problem-free. She will have her semi-annual, and sometimes burdensome, heat cycle after she is eight or nine months old. At these times she must be confined so that she will not soil her surroundings, and she must also be closely watched to prevent male dogs from gaining access to her or she will become pregnant.

ALTERING
Spaying the female or neutering the male will not change the personality of your pet and will avoid many problems. Neutering the male Pointer can reduce, if not entirely eliminate, its desire to pursue a neighbourhood female that shows signs of an impending romantic attitude.

Neutering and spaying also precludes the possibility of your Pointer adding to the pet overpopulation problem that concerns environmentalists world-wide. Altering also reduces the risk of mammary cancer in the female and testicular and prostate cancer in the male.

HEALTH CONCERNS
With a little luck and grace, the well-cared-for Pointer often lives to be 12 to 14 years

HIGH-ENERGY DOG
Pointers are not the best choices as companions for those who live either in a flat or in a city. Hundreds of years have been invested in making the Pointer a wide-ranging, highly energetic dog, and confining the Pointer to close quarters for long periods of time is likely to produce a neurotic, destructive and unhappy animal.

of age, acting hale and hearty for most of those years. Unfortunately, all breeds of domesticated dogs suffer from some hereditary problems, though the Pointer's problems are relatively few.

Probably the chief concern among Pointer breeders is hip dysplasia, commonly referred to as HD. This is a developmental disease of the hip joint. One or both hip joints of the

DO YOU KNOW ABOUT HIP DYSPLASIA?

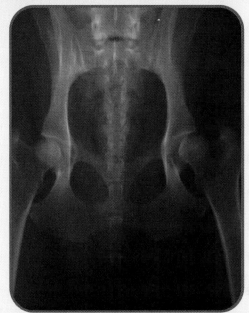

X-ray of a dog with 'Good' hips.

X-ray of a dog with 'Moderate' dysplastic hips.

Hip dysplasia is a fairly common condition found in purebred dogs. When a dog has hip dysplasia, its hind leg has an incorrectly formed hip joint. By constant use of the hip joint, it becomes more and more loose, wears abnormally and may become arthritic.

Hip dysplasia can only be confirmed with an x-ray, but certain symptoms may indicate a problem. Your dog may have a hip dysplasia problem if it walks in a peculiar manner, hops instead of smoothly runs, uses his hind legs in unison (to keep the pressure off the weak joint), has trouble getting up from a prone position or always sits with both legs together on one side of its body.

As the dog matures, it may adapt well to life with a bad hip, but in a few years the arthritis develops and many dogs with hip dysplasia become cripples.

Hip dysplasia is considered an inherited disease and only can be diagnosed definitively when the dog is two years old. Some experts claim that a special diet might help your puppy outgrow the bad hip, but the usual treatments are surgical. The removal of the pectineus muscle, the removal of the round part of the femur, reconstructing the pelvis and replacing the hip with an artificial one are all surgical interventions that are expensive, but they are usually very successful. Follow the advice of your veterinary surgeon.

affected dog have abnormal contours. Some dogs might show tenderness in the hip, walk with a limp or swaying gait or experience difficulty getting up. Symptoms vary from mild temporary lameness to severe crippling in extreme cases. Treatment may require surgery. Even though hip dysplasia is not very common in the Pointer, enough cases have been reported to merit asking the breeder of your puppy what testing he has done in respect to the problem.

Some occasions of a relatively rare and unusual disease known as neurotropic osteopathy have been documented in the breed. What appear to be skeletal injuries occur somewhere in the age range of three to nine months as a result of degeneration of the spinal cord.

There are reports of some skin problems, including demodectic mange. Regular grooming procedures are important in that they prevent any of these skin problems from progressing to an advanced stage.

Eye problems such as entropion and progressive retinal atrophy have been recorded by careful breeders, but not on an alarming basis. Here again, purchasing a Pointer from a respected breeder is extremely important.

INTRODUCTION TO THE CHILDREN

There is no better place to purchase a Pointer puppy destined for the role of family companion than one born and raised in a home atmosphere. This is particularly so if there are children in the household in which the puppy spends its first weeks. This introduces the puppy to the sights, sounds and variety of people with whom it will be spending its entire life.

Breed Standard for the

POINTER

The Pointer of the proper shape, balance and proportion creates a picture of a lithe elegant dog of noble carriage, able to perform in the field with speed and agility, the whole day long if necessary. The question that arises, however, is what tells us if a Pointer does, in fact, have the right make and shape, balance and proportion?

The answers to all this are found in The Kennel Club's breed standard. Breed standards are very accurate descriptions of the ideal specimen of a given breed. Standards describe the dog physically, listing all of a breed's anatomical parts and indicating how those parts should look. The standard also describes the breed's temperament and how it should move.

The standard is the blueprint which breeders use to fashion their breeding programmes. The

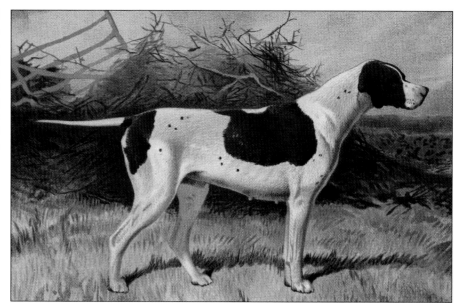

The famous Lloyd Price's Pointer, named Wragg. This painting was published in 1881 and is an interesting comparison to the Pointers of today.

goal, of course, is to move one step closer to that ever-elusive picture of perfection with each succeeding generation. A breed standard is also what dog show judges use to see which of the dogs being shown compares most favourably to what is required of a breed.

It should be understood that what the standard describes is the perfect dog of a given breed. In nature, nothing is absolutely perfect. Thus, the breeder and the judge are looking for the dog that, in their opinion, comes closest to that image of perfection. How each individual person interprets this standard will vary somewhat and no dog will possess every desired characteristic.

Although it takes many years to fully understand the implications of a breed standard, owners of Pointers should familiarise themselves with the stated requirements of the breed. This will enable the person who wishes to own a dog of that breed to have a good idea of what a representative specimen should look like.

THE KENNEL CLUB STANDARD FOR THE POINTER

General Appearance: Symmetrical and well built all over, general outline a series of graceful curves. A strong but lissom appearance.

A modern champion, Ch Kinnike Mickey of True Colors.

Characteristics: Aristocratic. Alert with appearance of strength, endurance and speed.

Temperament: Kind, even disposition.

Head and Skull: Skull of medium breadth, in proportion to length of foreface, stop well defined, pronounced occipital bone. Nose and eye rims dark, but may be lighter in the case of a lemon and white coloured dog. Nostrils wide, soft and moist. Muzzle somewhat

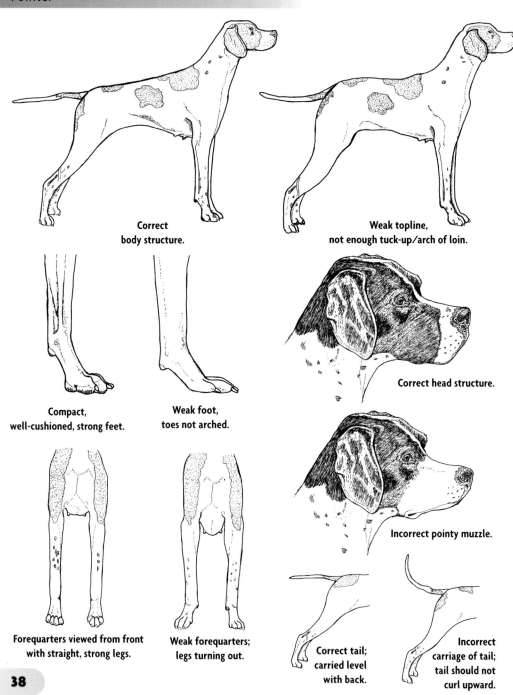

Correct
body structure.

Weak topline,
not enough tuck-up/arch of loin.

Compact,
well-cushioned, strong feet.

Weak foot,
toes not arched.

Correct head structure.

Forequarters viewed from front
with straight, strong legs.

Weak forequarters;
legs turning out.

Incorrect pointy muzzle.

Correct tail;
carried level
with back.

Incorrect
carriage of tail;
tail should not
curl upward.

concave, ending on level with nostrils, giving a slightly dish-faced appearance. Slight depression under eyes, cheek bones not prominent, well developed soft lip.

Eyes: Same distance from occiput as from nostrils, bright and kindly in expression. Either hazel or brown according to colour of coat. Neither bold nor staring, not looking down the nose.

Ears: Leathers thin, set on fairly high, lying close to head, of medium length, slightly pointed at tips.

Mouth: Jaws strong, with perfect, regular and complete scissor bite, i.e. upper teeth closely overlapping lower teeth and set square to the jaws.

Neck: Long, muscular, slightly arched, springing cleanly from shoulders and free from throatiness.

Forequarters: Shoulders long, sloping and well laid back. Chest just wide enough for plenty of heart room. Brisket well let down, to level with elbows. Forelegs straight and firm, with good oval bone, with back sinews strong and visible. Knee joint flat with front

Ch Kinnike Justin is in top condition, showing the typical Pointer pose. Notice the dog's overall musculature, especially evident in the chest and legs.

Lemon-and-white and black-and-white are two of the usual colour combinations seen in Pointers.

leg and protruding very little on inside. Pasterns lengthy, strong and resilient. Slightly sloping.

Body: Well sprung ribs carried well back gradually falling away at strong muscular and slightly arched loins. Short-coupled. Haunch bones well spaced and prominent, not above level of back.

Hindquarters: Very muscular. Well turned stifles. Good expanse of first and second thigh. Hocks well let down.

Feet: Oval, well knit, arched toes, well cushioned.

Tail: Medium length, thick at root, tapering gradually to a point. Well covered with close hair, carried on a level with back, with no upward curl. In movement, tail should lash from side to side.

Gait/Movement: Smooth, covering plenty of ground. Driving hind action, elbows neither in nor out. Definitely not a hackney action.

Coat: Fine, short, hard and evenly distributed, perfectly smooth and straight with decided sheen.

Colour: Usual colours are lemon and white, orange and white, liver and white, and black and white. Self colours and tricolours are also correct.

Size: Desirable heights at withers: dogs: 63–69 cms (25–27 ins); bitches: 61–66 cms (24–26 ins).

Faults: Any departure from the foregoing points should be considered a fault and the seriousness with which the fault should be regarded should be in exact proportion to its degree.

Note: Male animals should have two apparently normal testicles fully descended into the scrotum.

BREEDER'S BLUEPRINT

If you are considering breeding your bitch, it is very important that you are familiar with the breed standard. Reputable breeders breed with the intention of producing dogs that are as close as possible to the standard, and contribute to the advancement of the breed. Study the standard for both physical appearance and temperament, and make certain your bitch and your chosen stud dog measure up.

Even at nine years of age, Ch Kinnike Mannah is a winner in the show ring. Pictured here is a Best of Breed win.

BEST OF BREED

OX RIDGE KENNEL CLUB

SEPT. 19, 1992

Your Puppy
POINTER

HOW TO SELECT
A POINTER PUPPY

Your Pointer will live with you for many years. Therefore it is extremely important that the dog comes from a source where physical and mental soundness are primary considerations in the breeding programme, usually the result of careful breeding over a period of many years.

Although breeders of Pointers destined primarily for the show ring or as companions take pride in the fact that what they breed has not lost the hunting instinct, other factors are also considered when their breeding stock is selected. Amiability, points of conformation, and willingness to keep enthusiasm in check are examples of such desirable characteristics. A good question to ask the breeder of the puppy you are considering is why he breeds. A responsible breeder will have definite reasons for having produced a litter. The reasons could be varied because the Pointer is a very adaptable breed suitable for many purposes. However, if you suspect that the breeder breeds only to sell puppies, it is most advisable that you look elsewhere.

Visiting a breeder's home or kennel gives the buyer the distinct advantage of seeing the parents, or at least the mother of the puppies that are available. They normally have other relatives of the dog you are interested in on the premises as well.

Experienced breeders know which hereditary problems exist in the breed and will be willing to discuss them with you. Practically all breeds are subject to inherited conditions and Pointers are no exception. Beware of breeders who tell you that their dogs are not susceptible to inherited diseases or potential problems. We do not mean to imply that all Pointers are afflicted with genetic problems, but a reliable breeder will give you the information you are entitled to know regarding the individual you are considering.

Inspect the environment in which the dogs are raised. Cleanliness is the first clue that tells you how much the breeder cares about the dogs he or she owns. Cleanliness is as important to producing good stock as are good pedigrees. The time you spend in researching and inspecting the kennel will save you a great deal of money and heartache in the years to come.

Above all, the Pointer puppy you buy should be a happy, playful extrovert. Never select a puppy that appears sickly because you feel sorry for it and feel you will be able to nurse it back to good health. Well-bred Pointer puppies with positive temperaments are not afraid of strangers. You should not settle for anything less. Under normal circumstances you will have the whole litter in your lap if you kneel and call them to you.

Check inside the puppy's ears. They should be pink and clean. Any odour or dark discharge could indicate ear mites which, in turn, would indicate poor maintenance. The inside of the puppy's mouth and gums should be pink, and the teeth should be clean and white. There should be no malformation of the mouth or jaw. The eyes should be clear and bright. Again, be aware of any signs of discharge. The nose of a Pointer

PREPARING FOR PUP

Unfortunately, when a puppy is bought by someone who does not take into consideration the time and attention that dog ownership requires, it is the puppy who suffers when he is either abandoned or placed in a shelter by a frustrated owner. So all of the 'homework' you do in preparation for your pup's arrival will benefit you both. The more informed you are, the more you will know what to expect and the better equipped you will be to handle the ups and downs of raising a puppy. Hopefully, everyone in the household is willing to do his part in raising and caring for the pup. The anticipation of owning a dog often brings a lot of promises from excited family members: 'I will walk him every day,' 'I will feed him,' 'I will housebreak him,' etc., but these things take time and effort, and promises can easily be forgotten once the novelty of the new pet has worn off.

life-long problems.

If you have been reading and doing your research, you can expect the Pointer puppy to look somewhat like a miniaturised version of an adult. Of course, the puppy will not have the elegance and muscularity of a mature dog but all the basics will be there. The puppy's feet may well appear too big for the rest of its anatomy and the ears may seem bigger than they need be, but these are things the youngster will grow into as time passes.

The purchase of any dog is an important step since the well-cared-for dog will live with you for many years. In the case of a Pointer this could easily be 12 years or more, years both of you will want to enjoy. Therefore, it is extremely important in this breed that your Pointer is purchased from a breeder who has earned a reputation over the

puppy should never be crusted or running.

Pointer puppies should feel compact and substantial to the touch, never bony and undernourished, nor should they be bloated; a taut and bloated abdomen is usually a sign of worms. A rounded puppy belly is normal. Coughing or signs of diarrhoea are danger signals as are skin eruptions.

Conformation is important even at an early age. One should remember that the Pointer was originally bred to work in the field the whole day long. Even if the Pointer you buy will never hear a gun or be required to perform as a hunter, the puppy's movement should still be free from impediment. Limping or stumbling could easily mean

PUPPY APPEARANCE

Your puppy should have a well-fed appearance but not a distended abdomen, which may indicate worms or incorrect feeding, or both. The body should be firm, with a solid feel. The skin of the abdomen should be pale pink and clean, without signs of scratching or rash. Check the hind legs to make certain that dewclaws were removed, if any were present at birth.

years for consistently producing dogs which are mentally and physically sound. Not only is a sound and stable temperament of paramount importance in a large breed of this kind, but also there are health concerns which exist in the breed that good breeders are constantly aware of and do their utmost to eliminate.

Unfortunately, the buyer must beware. There are always those who are ready and willing to exploit a breed for financial gain with no thought given to its health or welfare, or to the homes in which the dogs will be living.

The only way a breeder can earn a reputation for producing quality animals is through a well-thought-out breeding programme in which rigid selectivity is imposed. Selective breeding aims at maintaining the virtues of a breed and eliminating genetic weaknesses. This process is time-consuming and costly. Therefore, responsible Pointer breeders protect their investment by providing the utmost in prenatal care for their brood matrons and maximum care and nutrition for the resulting offspring. Once the puppies arrive, the knowledgeable breeder initiates a proper socialisation process.

The Kennel Club or a local dog club will be happy to direct a prospective dog buyer to responsible breeders of quality stock. Should you not know where to contact a respected breeder in your area, we strongly recommend contacting the local Pointer club (if one exists) or The Kennel Club (or your country's governing kennel club) for recommendations.

Selecting a Pointer puppy starts with selecting a breeder and observing the litter.

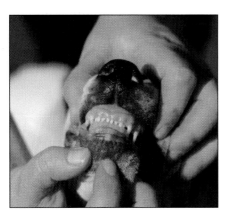

Pointer puppy, showing correct bite. A Pointer should have a scissor bite, meaning that the upper teeth closely overlap the lower teeth.

It is extremely important that the buyer knows the character and quality of a puppy's parents. Good temperament and good health are inherited and if the puppy's parents are not sound in these respects there is not much likelihood that they will produce offspring that are. Never buy a Pointer from anyone who has no first-hand knowledge of the puppy's parents or what kind of care a puppy has received since birth.

SHOW DOG, COMPANION OR HUNTER?

We have discussed the primary characteristics of the happy, healthy puppy that will fit the bill as companion and member of the family. However, if you want to be assured of a dog that will be of real show quality, then the fact that the puppy comes from stock known to produce the necessary qualities becomes a major consideration. Also, the

older the puppy is at the time of selection, the more likely you will know how good a dog you will have at maturity. The most any breeder can say about an eight-week-old Pointer puppy is that it has or does not have show or field potential.

If the excitement and pride of owning a winning show dog or outstanding hunting companion appeal to you, we strongly urge you to find a successful breeder who has a record of having produced dogs that have been successful in these endeavours through the years.

COMMITMENT OF OWNERSHIP

After considering all of these factors, you have most likely already made some very

DOCUMENTATION

Two important documents you will get from the breeder are the pup's pedigree and registration certificate. The breeder should register the litter and each pup with The Kennel Club, and it is necessary for you to have the paperwork if you plan on showing or breeding in the future.

Make sure you know the breeder's intentions on which type of registration he will obtain for the pup. There are limited registrations which may prohibit the dog from being shown, bred or from competing in non-conformation trials such as Working or Agility if the breeder feels that the pup is not of sufficient quality to do so. There is also a type of registration that will permit the dog in non-conformation competition only.

On the reverse side of the registration certificate, the new owner can find the transfer section which must be signed by the breeder.

PUPPY SELECTION

Your selection of a good puppy can be determined by your needs. A show potential or a good pet? It is your choice. Every puppy, however, should be of good temperament. Although show-quality puppies are bred and raised with emphasis on physical conformation, responsible breeders strive for equally good temperament. Do not buy from a breeder who concentrates solely on physical beauty at the expense of personality.

important decisions about selecting your puppy. You have chosen a Pointer, which means that you have decided which characteristics you want in a dog and what type of dog will best fit into your family and lifestyle. If you have selected a breeder, you have gone a step further—you have done your research and found a responsible, conscientious person who breeds quality Pointers and who should be a reliable source of help as

YOUR SCHEDULE . . .

If you lead an erratic, unpredictable life, with daily or weekly changes in your work requirements, consider the problems of owning a puppy. The new puppy has to be fed regularly, socialised (loved, petted, handled, introduced to other people) and, most importantly, allowed to visit outdoors for toilet training. As the dog gets older, it can be more tolerant of deviations in its feeding and toilet relief.

you and your puppy adjust to life together. If you have observed a litter in action, you have obtained a firsthand look at the dynamics of a puppy 'pack' and, thus, you should learn about each pup's individual personality—perhaps you have even found one that particularly appeals to you.

However, even if you have not yet found the Pointer puppy of your dreams, observing pups will help you learn to recognise certain behaviour and to determine what a pup's behaviour indicates about his temperament. You will be able to pick out which pups are the leaders, which ones are less outgoing, which ones are confident, which ones are shy, playful, friendly, aggressive, etc. Equally as important, you will learn to recognise what a healthy pup should look and act like. All of these things will help you in your search, and when you find the Pointer that was meant for you, you will know it!

Researching your breed, selecting a responsible breeder and observing as many pups as possible are all important steps on the way to dog ownership. It may seem like a lot of effort... and you have not even taken the pup home yet! Remember, though, you cannot be too careful when it comes to deciding on the type of dog you want and finding out about your prospective pup's background. Buying a puppy is not—or should not be—just another whimsical purchase. This is one instance in which you actually do get to choose your own family! You may be thinking that buying a puppy should be fun—it should not be so serious and so much work. Keep in mind that your puppy is not a cuddly stuffed toy or decorative lawn ornament, but a creature that will become a real member of your family. You will come to realise that, while buying a puppy is a pleasurable and exciting endeavour, it is not something to be taken lightly. Relax...the fun will start when the pup comes home!

Always keep in mind that a puppy is nothing more than a baby in a furry disguise...a baby who is virtually helpless in a human world and who trusts his owner for fulfilment of his basic needs for survival. In addition to water and shelter, your pup needs care, protection, guidance and love. If you are not prepared

DID YOU KNOW?

Breeders rarely release puppies until they are eight to ten weeks of age. This is an acceptable age for most breeds of dog, excepting toy breeds, which are not released until around 12 weeks, given their petite sizes. If a breeder has a puppy that is 12 weeks or more, it is likely well socialised and housetrained. Be sure that it is otherwise healthy before deciding to take it home.

ARE YOU A FIT OWNER?

If the breeder from whom you are buying a puppy asks you a lot of personal questions, do not be insulted. Such a breeder wants to be sure that you will be a fit provider for his puppy.

to commit to this, then you are not prepared to own a dog.

Wait a minute, you say. How hard could this be? All of my neighbours own dogs and they seem to be doing just fine. Why should I have to worry about all of this? Well, you should not

49

QUALITY FOOD

The cost of food must also be mentioned. All dogs need a good quality food with an adequate supply of protein to develop their bones and muscles properly. Most dogs are not picky eaters but unless fed properly they can quickly succumb to skin problems.

PREPARING PUPPY'S PLACE IN YOUR HOME

Researching your breed and finding a breeder are only two aspects of the 'homework' you will have to do before taking your Pointer puppy home. You will also have to prepare your home and family for the new addition. Much as you would prepare a nursery for a newborn baby, you will need to designate a place in your home that will be the puppy's own. How you prepare your home will depend on how much freedom the dog will be allowed. Whatever you decide, you must ensure that he has a place that he can 'call his own.'

When you bring your new puppy into your home, you are bringing him into what will become his home as well. Obviously, you did not buy a puppy so that he could take over your house, but in order for a puppy to grow into a stable, well-adjusted dog, he has to feel

worry about it; in fact, you will probably find that once your Pointer pup gets used to his new home, he will fall into his place in the family quite naturally. But it never hurts to emphasise the commitment of dog ownership. With some time and patience, it is really not too difficult to raise a curious and exuberant Pointer pup to be a well-adjusted and well-mannered adult dog—a dog that could be your most loyal friend.

BOY OR GIRL?

An important consideration to be discussed is the sex of your puppy. For a family companion, a bitch may be the better choice, considering the female's inbred concern for all young creatures and her accompanying tolerance and patience. It is always advisable to spay a pet bitch, which may guarantee her a longer life.

comfortable in his surroundings. Remember, he is leaving the warmth and security of his mother and littermates, as well as the familiarity of the only place he has ever known, so it is important to make his transition as easy as possible. By preparing a place in your home for the puppy, you are making him feel as welcome as possible in a strange new place. It should not take him long to get used to it, but the sudden shock of being transplanted is somewhat traumatic for a young pup. Imagine how a small child would feel in the same situation—that is how your puppy must be feeling. It is up to you to reassure him and to let him know, 'Little chap, you are going to like it here!'

WHAT YOU SHOULD BUY

CRATE

To someone unfamiliar with the use of crates in dog training, it may seem like punishment to shut a dog in a crate, but this is not the case at all. Although all breeders do not advocate crate training, more and more breeders and trainers are recommending crates as preferred tools for show puppies as well as pet puppies. Crates are not cruel—crates have many humane and highly effective uses in dog care and training.

For example, crate training is a very popular and very successful housebreaking method. A crate can keep your dog safe during

FEEDING TIP
You will probably start feeding your pup the same food that he has been getting from the breeder; the breeder should give you a few days' supply to start you off. Although you should not give your pup too many treats, you will want to have puppy treats on hand for coaxing, training, rewards, etc. Be careful, though, as a small pup's calorie requirements are relatively low and a few treats can add up to almost a full day's worth of calories without the required nutrition.

Your local pet shop will have a supply of crates in different sizes and styles. Since the crate is a purchase that should last for the dog's lifetime, get a high-quality crate that is large enough for the fully grown Pointer.

PHOTO COURTESY OF DOSKOCIL.

little more luxurious than what his early ancestors enjoyed.

As far as purchasing a crate, the type that you buy is up to you. It will most likely be one of the two most popular types: wire or fibreglass. There are advantages and disadvantages to each type. For example, a wire crate is more open, allowing the air to flow through and affording the dog a view of what is going on around him while a fibreglass crate is sturdier. Both can double as travel crates, providing protection for the dog. The size of the crate is another thing to consider. Puppies do not stay puppies forever—in fact, sometimes it seems as if they grow right before your eyes. A small-sized crate may be fine for a very young Pointer pup, but it will not do him much good for long! Unless you have the money and the inclination to buy a new crate every time your pup has a growth spurt, it is better to get one that will accommodate your dog both as a pup and at full size. A large-size crate will be necessary for a full-grown Pointer, who stands approximately 27 inches high.

BEDDING
Veterinary bedding in the dog's crate will help the dog feel more at home and you may also like to pop in a small blanket. This will take the place of the leaves,

travel and, perhaps most importantly, a crate provides your dog with a place of his own in your home. It serves as a 'doggie bedroom' of sorts—your Pointer can curl up in his crate when he wants to sleep or when he just needs a break. Many dogs sleep in their crates overnight. With soft bedding and his favourite toy, a crate becomes a cosy pseudo-den for your dog. Like his ancestors, he too will seek out the comfort and retreat of a den—you just happen to be providing him with something a

twigs, etc., that the pup would use in the wild to make a den; the pup can make his own 'burrow' in the crate. Although your pup is far removed from his den-making ancestors, the denning instinct is still a part of his genetic makeup. Second, until you take your pup home, he has been sleeping amidst the warmth of his mother and litter-mates, and while a blanket is not the same as a warm, breathing body, it still provides heat and something with which to snuggle. You will want to wash your pup's bedding frequently in case he has an accident in his

A wire crate can easily be disassembled for transport, and it allows the dog a view of what's going on around him. Wire crates are often preferred for use in the home.

crate, and replace or remove any blanket that becomes ragged and starts to fall apart.

Toys

Toys are a must for dogs of all ages, especially for curious playful pups. Puppies are the 'children' of the dog world, and what child does not love toys? Chew toys provide enjoyment for both dog and owner—your dog will enjoy playing with his favourite toys, while you will enjoy the fact that they distract him from your expensive shoes and leather sofa. Puppies love to chew; in fact, chewing is a physical need for pups as they are teething, and everything

In addition to the crate, you can purchase a dog bed for your Pointer. Also make certain to bring home plenty of safe chew toys.

CRATE TRAINING TIPS

During crate training, you should partition off the section of the crate in which the pup stays. If he is given too big an area, this will hinder your training efforts. Crate training is based on the fact that a dog does not like to soil his sleeping quarters, so it is ineffective to keep a pup in a crate that is so big that he can eliminate in one end and get far enough away from it to sleep. Also, you want to make the crate den-like for the pup. Blankets and a favourite toy will make the crate cosy for the small pup; as he grows, you may want to evict some of his 'roommates' to make more room.

It will take some coaxing at first, but be patient. Given some time to get used to it, your pup will adapt to his new home-within-a-home quite nicely.

looks appetising! The full range of your possessions—from old tea towel to Oriental carpet—are fair game in the eyes of a teething pup. Puppies are not all that discerning when it comes to finding something to literally 'sink their teeth into'— everything tastes great!

Pointer puppies are aggressive chewers and only the hardest, strongest toys should be offered to them. Breeders advise owners to resist stuffed toys, because they can become de-stuffed in no time. The overly excited pup may ingest the stuffing, which is neither digestible nor nutritious.

Similarly, squeaky toys are quite popular, but must be avoided for the Pointer. Perhaps a squeaky toy can be used as an aid in training, but not for free play. If a pup 'disembowels' one of these, the small plastic squeaker inside can be dangerous if swallowed. Monitor the condition of all your pup's toys carefully and get rid of any that have been chewed to the point of becoming potentially dangerous.

Be careful of natural bones, which have a tendency to splinter into sharp, dangerous pieces. Also be careful of rawhide, which can turn into

Pointers are chewers and teething puppies will chew on anything they can get their teeth into. Supply your pup with a variety of durable chew toys, for his safety and the safety of your belongings.

pieces that are easy to swallow and become a mushy mess on your carpet.

Pointers can become problem chewers if not given sufficient exercise to take the edge off their energy level. Be certain to offer your Pointer high-resistance chew toys and give him plenty of exercise to avoid a chewing problem from occurring.

LEAD

A nylon lead is probably the best option as it is the most resistant to puppy teeth should your pup take a liking to chewing on his lead. Of course, this is a habit that should be nipped in the bud, but if your pup likes to chew on his lead he has a very slim chance of being able to chew through the strong nylon. Nylon leads are also lightweight, which is good for a young Pointer who is just getting used to the idea of walking on a lead. For everyday walking and safety purposes, the nylon lead is a good choice. As your pup grows up and gets used to walking on the lead, you may want to purchase a flexible lead. These leads allow you to extend the length to give the dog a broader area to explore or to shorten the length to keep the dog near you. Of course there are special leads for training purposes, and specially made leather

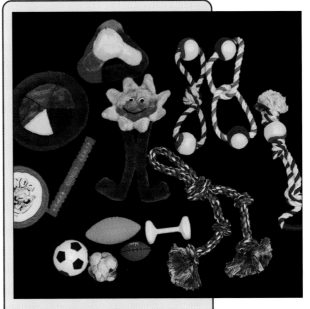

TOYS, TOYS, TOYS!
With a big variety of dog toys available, and so many that look like they would be a lot of fun for a dog, be careful in your selection. It is amazing what a set of puppy teeth can do to an innocent-looking toy, so, obviously, safety is a major consideration. Be sure to choose the most durable products that you can find. Hard nylon bones and toys are a safe bet, and many of them are offered in different scents and flavours that will be sure to capture your dog's attention. It is always fun to play a game of catch with your dog, and there are balls and flying discs that are specially made to withstand dog teeth.

Your local pet shop will have a large variety of collars and leads from which you can make a selection.

harnesses, but these are not necessary for routine walks.

COLLAR

Your pup should get used to wearing a collar all the time since you will want to attach his ID tags to it. You have to attach the lead to something! A lightweight nylon collar is a good choice; make sure that it fits snugly enough so that the pup cannot wriggle out of it, but is loose enough so that it will not be uncomfortably tight

The collar should fit snugly around your Pointer's neck and should have the dog's ID tags securely attached.

around the pup's neck. You should be able to fit a finger between the pup and the collar. It may take some time for your pup to get used to wearing the collar, but soon he will not even notice that it is there. Choke collars are made for training, but should only be used by an experienced handler.

FOOD AND WATER BOWLS

Your pup will need two bowls, one for food and one for water. You may want two sets of bowls, one for inside and one for outside, depending on where the dog will be fed and where he will be spending time. Stainless steel or sturdy plastic bowls are popular choices. Plastic bowls are more chewable. Dogs tend not to chew on the steel variety, which can be sterilised. It is important to buy sturdy bowls since anything is in danger of being chewed by puppy teeth and you do not want your dog to be constantly chewing apart his bowl (for his safety and for your purse!).

CLEANING SUPPLIES

Until a pup is housetrained you will be doing a lot of cleaning. Accidents will occur, which is acceptable in the beginning because the puppy does not know any better. All you can do is be prepared to clean up any 'accidents.' Old rags, towels,

Food and water bowls are made in a variety of materials, including plastic, pottery and stainless steel.

PHOTO COURTESY OF MIKKI PET PRODUCTS.

CHOOSING THE RIGHT COLLAR

The BUCKLE COLLAR is the standard collar used for everyday purpose. Be sure that you adjust the buckle on growing puppies. Check it every day. It can become too tight overnight! These collars can be made of leather or nylon. Attach your dog's identification tags to this collar.

The CHOKE COLLAR is the usual collar recommended for training. It is constructed of highly polished steel so that it slides easily through the stainless steel loop. The idea is that the dog controls the pressure around its neck and he will stop pulling if the collar becomes uncomfortable. Never leave a choke collar on your dog when not training.

The HALTER is for a trained dog that has to be restrained to prevent running away, chasing a cat and the like. Considered the most humane of all collars, it is frequently used on smaller dogs for which collars are not comfortable.

Cleaning up after your dog is a must. Your local pet shop has various devices that make the task less onerous.

newspapers and a safe disinfectant are good to have on hand.

BEYOND THE BASICS
The items previously discussed are the bare necessities. You will find out what else you need as you go along—grooming supplies, flea/tick protection, baby gates to partition a room, etc. These things will vary depending on your situation but it is important that you have everything you need to feed and make your Pointer comfortable in his first few days at home.

PUPPY-PROOFING
Aside from ensuring that your Pointer will be comfortable in your home, you also have to

PUPPY-PROOFING
Thoroughly puppy-proof your house before bringing your puppy home. Never use roach or rodent poisons in any area accessible to the puppy. Avoid the use of toilet cleaners. Most dogs are born with 'toilet sonar' and will take a drink if the lid is left open. Also keep the rubbish secured and out of reach.

make certain that your home is safe for your Pointer. This means taking precautions that your pup will not get into anything he should not get into and that there is nothing within his reach that may harm him should he sniff it, chew it, inspect it, etc. This probably seems obvious since, while you are primarily

he is to be limited to certain places within the house, keep any potentially dangerous items in the 'off-limits' areas. An electrical cord can pose a danger should the puppy decide to taste it—and who is going to convince a pup that it would not make a great chew toy? Cords should be fastened tightly against the wall. If your dog is going to spend time in a crate, make sure that there is nothing near his crate that he can reach if he sticks his curious little nose or paws through the openings. Just as you would with a child, keep all household cleaners and chemicals where the pup cannot reach them.

It is also important to make sure that the outside of your home is safe. Of course your puppy should never be unsupervised, but a pup let loose in the garden will want to run and explore, and he should be granted that freedom. Do not let

This Pointer pup has found some new friends to snuggle with and keep him warm.

concerned with your pup's safety, at the same time you do not want your belongings to be ruined. Breakables should be placed out of reach if your dog is to have full run of the house. If

DO YOUR HOMEWORK!
In order to know whether or not a puppy will fit into your lifestyle, you need to assess his personality. A good way to do this is to interact with his parents. Your pup inherits not only his appearance but also his personality and temperament from the sire and dam. If the parents are fearful or overly aggressive, these same traits may likely show up in your puppy.

a fence give you a false sense of security; you would be surprised how crafty (and persistent) a dog can be in working out how to dig under and squeeze his way through small holes. Fortunately Pointers are not climbers and rarely will try to climb over a fence, but jumping is one of the Pointer's finer skills. Curious and cunning, a Pointer is always interested in seeing what is on the other side of the mountain and once loose, it is amazing how quickly they can get there. The remedy is to make the fence

CHEMICAL TOXINS
Scour your garage for potential puppy dangers. Remove weed killers, pesticides and antifreeze materials. Antifreeze is highly toxic and even a few drops can kill an adult dog. The sweet taste attracts the animal, who will quickly consume it from the floor or curbside.

well embedded into the ground and high enough so that it really is impossible for your dog to get over it (about 3 metres should suffice). Be sure to repair or secure any gaps in the fence. Check the fence periodically to ensure that it is in good shape and make repairs as needed; a very determined pup may return to the same spot to 'work on it' until he is able to get through.

FIRST TRIP TO THE VET
You have selected your puppy, and your home and family are ready. Now all you have to do is collect your Pointer from the breeder and the fun begins, right? Well...not so fast. Something else you need to prepare is your pup's first trip to the veterinary surgeon. Perhaps the breeder can recommend someone in the area that specialises in hunting or gun dogs, or maybe you know some other Pointer owners who can suggest a good vet. Either way, you should have an appointment

Puppies will investigate...it's just part of being a puppy! Supervise your pup to keep him out of danger, and keep any potentially harmful items out of his reach.

PLAY'S THE THING

Teaching the puppy to play with his toys in running and fetching games is an ideal way to help the puppy develop muscle, learn motor skills and bond with you his owner and master.

He also needs to learn how to inhibit his bite reflex and never to use his teeth on people, forbidden objects and other animals in play. Whenever you play with your puppy, you make the rules. This becomes an important message to your puppy in teaching him that you are the pack leader and control everything he does in life. Once your dog accepts you as his leader, your relationship with him will be cemented for life.

arranged for your pup before you pick him up.

The pup's first visit will consist of an overall examination to make sure that the pup does not have any problems that are not apparent to the eye. The veterinary surgeon will also set up a schedule for the pup's vaccinations; the breeder will inform you of which ones the pup has already received and the vet can continue from there.

INTRODUCTION TO THE FAMILY

Everyone in the house will be excited about the puppy coming home and will want to pet him and play with him, but it is best to make the introduction low-key so as not to overwhelm the puppy. He is apprehensive already. It is the first time he has been separated from his mother and the breeder, and the ride to your home is likely to be the first time he has been in a car. The last thing you want to do is smother him, as this will only frighten him further. This is not to say that human contact is not extremely necessary at this stage, because this is the time when a connection between the pup and his human family is formed. Gentle petting and soothing words should help console him, as well as just putting him down and letting him explore on his own (under your watchful eye, of course).

The pup may approach the family members or may busy himself with exploring for a while. Gradually, each person

NATURAL TOXINS

Examine your grass and garden landscaping before bringing your puppy home. Many varieties of plants have leaves, stems or flowers that are toxic if ingested, and you can depend on a curious puppy to investigate them. Ask your vet for information on poisonous plants or research them at your library.

TRAVEL TIP

Taking your dog from the breeder to your home in a car can be a very uncomfortable experience for both of you. The puppy will have been taken from his warm, friendly, safe environment and brought into a strange new environment. An environment that moves! Be prepared for loose bowels, urination, crying, whining and even fear biting. With proper love and encouragement when you arrive home, the stress of the trip should quickly disappear.

should spend some time with the pup, one at a time, crouching down to get as close to the pup's level as possible and letting him sniff that person's hands and petting him gently. He definitely needs human attention and he needs to be touched—this is how to form an immediate bond. Just remember that the pup is experiencing a lot of things for the first time, at the same time. There are new people, new noises, new smells, and new things to investigate: so be gentle, be affectionate, and be as comforting as you can be.

When you bring your Pointer puppy home, everything will be new to him. Give him time to explore and get used to all of the sights, scents and sounds.

PUP'S FIRST NIGHT HOME
You have travelled home with your new charge safely in his crate. He's been to the vet for a thorough check-up; he's been weighed, his papers examined; perhaps he's even been vaccinated and wormed as well. He's met the family, licked the whole family, including the excited children and the less-than-happy cat. He's explored his area, his new bed, the garden and anywhere else he's been permitted. He's eaten his first meal at home and relieved himself in the proper place. He's heard lots of new sounds, smelled new friends and seen more of the outside world than ever before.

A FORTNIGHT'S GRACE
It will take at least two weeks for your puppy to become accustomed to his new surroundings. Give him lots of love, attention, handling, frequent opportunities to relieve himself, a diet he likes to eat and a place he can call his own.

That was just the first day! He's worn out and is ready for bed...or so you think!

It's puppy's first night and you are ready to say 'Good night'—keep in mind that this is puppy's first night ever to be sleeping alone. His dam and littermates are no longer at paw's length and he's a bit scared, cold and lonely. Be reassuring to your new family member. This is not the time to spoil him and give in to his inevitable whining.

Puppies whine. They whine to let others know where they are and hopefully to get company out of it. Place your pup in his new bed or crate in his room and close the door. Mercifully, he may fall asleep without a peep. When the inevitable occurs, ignore the whining: he is fine. Be strong and keep his interest in mind. Do not allow yourself to feel guilty and visit the pup. He will fall asleep eventually.

Many breeders recommend placing a piece of bedding from his former home in his new bed so that he recognises the scent of his littermates. Others still advise placing a hot water bottle in his bed for warmth. This latter may be a good idea provided the pup doesn't attempt to suckle—he'll get good and wet and may not fall asleep so fast.

Puppy's first night can be somewhat stressful for the pup and his new family. Remember that you are setting the tone of nighttime at your house. Unless you want to play with your pup every evening at 10 p.m., midnight and 2 a.m., don't initiate the habit. Your family will thank you, and so will your pup!

PREVENTING PUPPY PROBLEMS

SOCIALISATION

Now that you have done all of the preparatory work and have helped your pup get accustomed to his new home and family, it is about time for you to have some fun! Socialising your Pointer pup gives you the opportunity to show off your new friend, and your pup gets to reap the benefits of being an adorable furry creature that people will want to pet and, in general, think is absolutely precious!

Besides getting to know his new family, your puppy should be exposed to other people, animals and situations, but of course he must not come into close contact with dogs you don't know well until his course of injections is fully complete. This will help him become well adjusted as he grows up and less prone to being timid or fearful of the new things he will

TRAINING TIP

Training your puppy takes much patience and can be frustrating at times, but you should see results from your efforts. If you have a puppy that seems untrainable, take him to a trainer or behaviourist. The dog may have a personality problem that requires the help of a professional, or perhaps you need help in learning how to train your dog.

encounter. Your pup's socialisation began with the breeder but now it is your responsibility to continue it. The socialisation he receives up until the age of 12 weeks is the most critical, as this is the time when he forms his

Raised together since puppyhood, this Pointer and his Boston Terrier housemate are the best of friends.

him around the neighbourhood, take him on your daily errands, let people pet him, let him meet other dogs and pets, etc. Puppies do not have to try to make friends; there will be no shortage of people who will want to introduce themselves. Just make sure that you carefully supervise each meeting. If the neighbourhood children want to say hello, for example, that is great—children and pups most often make great companions. Sometimes an excited child can unintentionally handle a pup too roughly, or an overzealous pup can playfully nip a little too hard. You want to make socialisation experiences positive ones. What a pup learns during this very formative stage will affect his attitude toward future encounters. You want your dog to be comfortable around everyone. A pup that has a bad experience with a child may

impressions of the outside world. Be especially careful during the eight-to-ten-week period, also known as the fear period. The interaction he receives during this time should be gentle and reassuring. Lack of socialisation can manifest itself in fear and aggression as the dog grows up. He needs lots of human contact, affection, handling and exposure to other animals.

Once your pup has received his necessary vaccinations, feel free to take him out and about (on his lead, of course). Walk

SOCIALISATION
Thorough socialisation includes not only meeting new people but also being introduced to new experiences such as riding in the car, having his coat brushed, hearing the television, walking in a crowd—the list is endless. The more your pup experiences, and the more positive the experiences are, the less of a shock and the less frightening it will be for your pup to encounter new things.

grow up to be a dog that is shy around or aggressive toward children.

CONSISTENCY IN TRAINING

Dogs, being pack animals, naturally need a leader, or else they try to establish dominance in their packs. When you welcome a dog into your family, the choice of who becomes the leader and who becomes the 'pack' is entirely up to you! Your pup's intuitive quest for dominance, coupled with the fact that it is nearly impossible to look at an adorable Pointer pup with his 'puppy-dog' eyes and not cave in, give the pup almost an unfair advantage in getting the upper hand! A pup will definitely test the waters to see what he can and cannot do. Do not give in to those pleading eyes—stand your ground when it comes to disciplining the pup and make sure that all family members do the same. It will only confuse the pup when Mother tells him to get off the sofa when he is used to sitting up there with Father to watch the nightly news. Avoid discrepancies by having all members of the household decide on the rules before the pup even comes home…and be consistent in enforcing them! Early training shapes the dog's personality, so you cannot be unclear in what you expect.

MANNERS MATTER

During the socialisation process, a puppy should meet people, experience different environments and definitely be exposed to other canines. Through playing and interacting with other dogs, your puppy will learn lessons, ranging from controlling the pressure of his jaws by biting his litter mates to the inner-workings of the canine pack that he will apply to his human relationships for the rest of his life. That is why removing a puppy from its litter too early (before eight weeks) can be detrimental to the pup's development.

COMMON PUPPY PROBLEMS

The best way to prevent puppy problems is to be proactive in stopping an undesirable behaviour as soon as it starts. The old saying 'You can't teach an old dog new tricks' does not necessarily hold true, but it is true that it is much easier to discourage bad behaviour in a young developing pup than to wait until the pup's bad behaviour becomes the adult dog's bad habit. There are some problems that are especially prevalent in puppies as they develop.

NIPPING

As puppies start to teethe, they feel the need to sink their teeth into anything available... unfortunately that includes your fingers, arms, hair and toes. You may find this behaviour cute for the first five seconds...until you feel just how sharp those puppy teeth are. This is something you want to discourage immediately and consistently with a firm 'No!' (or whatever number of firm 'No's' it takes for him to understand that you mean business). Then replace your finger with an appropriate chew

> **PROPER SOCIALISATION**
> The socialisation period for puppies is from age 8 to 16 weeks. This is the time when puppies need to leave their birth family and take up residence with their new owners, where they will meet many new people, other pets, etc. Failure to be adequately socialised can cause the dog to grow up fearing others and being shy and unfriendly due to a lack of self-confidence.

toy. While this behaviour is merely annoying when the dog is young, it can become dangerous as your Pointer's adult teeth grow in and his jaws develop, and he continues to think it is okay to gnaw on human appendages. Your Pointer does not mean any harm with a friendly nip, but he also does not know his own strength.

CRYING/WHINING

Your pup will often cry, whine, whimper, howl or make some type of commotion when he is left alone. This is basically his way of calling out for attention to make sure that you know he is there and that you have not forgotten about him. He feels insecure when he is left alone, when you are out of the house and he is in his crate or when you are in another part of the

> **PUPPY PROBLEMS**
> The majority of problems that are commonly seen in young pups will disappear as your dog gets older. However, how you deal with problems when he is young will determine how he reacts to discipline as an adult dog. It is important to establish who is boss (hopefully it will be you!) right away when you are first bonding with your dog. This bond will set the tone for the rest of your life together.

house and he cannot see you. The noise he is making is an expression of the anxiety he feels at being alone, so he needs to be taught that being alone is okay. You are not actually training the dog to stop making noise, you are training him to feel comfortable when he is alone and thus removing the need for him to make the noise. This is where the crate with cosy bedding and a toy comes in handy. You want to know that he is safe when you are not there to supervise, and you know that he will be safe in his crate rather than roaming freely about the house. In order for the pup to stay in his crate without making a fuss, he needs to be comfortable in his crate. On that note, it is extremely important that the crate is never used as a form of punishment, or the pup will have a negative association with the crate.

Accustom the pup to the crate in short, gradually increasing time intervals in which you put him in the crate, maybe with a treat, and stay in the room with him. If he cries or makes a fuss, do not go to him, but stay in his sight. Gradually he will realise that staying in his crate is all right without your help, and it will not be so traumatic for him when you are not around. You may want to leave the radio on

CHEWING TIPS

Chewing goes hand in hand with nipping in the sense that a teething puppy is always looking for a way to soothe his aching gums. In this case, instead of chewing on you, he may have taken a liking to your favourite shoe or something else which he should not be chewing. Again, realise that this is a normal canine behaviour that does not need to be discouraged, only redirected. Your pup just needs to be taught what is acceptable to chew on and what is off limits. Consistently tell him NO when you catch him chewing on something forbidden and give him a chew toy. Conversely, praise him when you catch him chewing on something appropriate. In this way you are discouraging the inappropriate behaviour and reinforcing the desired behaviour. The puppy chewing should stop after his adult teeth have come in, but an adult dog continues to chew for various reasons—perhaps because he is bored, perhaps to relieve tension or perhaps he just likes to chew. That is why it is important to redirect his chewing when he is still young.

softly when you leave the house; the sound of human voices may be comforting to him.

DIETARY AND FEEDING CONSIDERATIONS

Today the choices of food for your Pointer are many and varied. There are simply dozens of brands of food in all sorts of flavours and textures, ranging from puppy diets to those for seniors. There are even hypoallergenic and low-calorie diets available. Because your Pointer's food has a bearing on coat, health and temperament, it is essential that the most suitable diet is selected for a Pointer of his age. It is fair to say, however, that even experienced owners can be perplexed by the enormous range of foods available. Only understanding what is best for your dog will help you reach a valued decision.

Dog foods are produced in three basic types: dried, semi-moist and tinned. Dried foods are useful for the cost-conscious for overall they tend to be less expensive than semi-moist or tinned. They also contain the least fat and the most preservatives. In general, tinned foods are made up of 60–70 percent water, while semi-moist ones often contain so much sugar that they are perhaps the least preferred by owners, even though their dogs seem to like them.

When selecting your dog's diet, three stages of development must be considered: the puppy stage, adult stage and the senior or veteran stage.

PUPPY STAGE

Puppies instinctively want to suck milk from their mother's teats and a normal puppy will

FEEDING TIP

You must store your dried dog food carefully. Open packages of dog food quickly lose their vitamin value, usually within 90 days of being opened. Mould spores and vermin could also contaminate the food.

exhibit this behaviour from just a few moments following birth. If puppies do not attempt to suckle within the first half-hour or so, they should be encouraged to do so by placing them on the nipples, having selected ones with plenty of milk. This early milk supply is important in providing colostrum to protect the puppies during the first eight to ten weeks of their lives. Although a mother's milk is much better than any milk formula, despite there being some excellent ones available, if the puppies do not feed, you will have to feed them yourself. For those with less experience, advice from a veterinary surgeon is important so that you feed not only the right quantity of milk but that of correct quality, fed at suitably frequent intervals, usually every two hours during the first few days of life.

Puppies should be allowed to nurse from their mothers for about the first six weeks, although from the third or fourth week you should begin to introduce small portions of suitable solid food. Most breeders like to introduce alternate milk and meat meals initially, building up to weaning time.

By the time the puppies are seven or a maximum of eight weeks old, they should be fully weaned and fed solely on a

FOOD PREFERENCE
Selecting the best dried dog food is difficult. There is no majority consensus among veterinary scientists as to the value of nutrient analyses (protein, fat, fibre, moisture, ash, cholesterol, minerals, etc.). All agree that feeding trials are what matters, but you also have to consider the individual dog. Its weight, age, activity and what pleases its taste, all must be considered. It is probably best to take the advice of your veterinary surgeon. Every dog's dietary requirements vary, even during the lifetime of a particular dog.

If your dog is fed a good dried food, it does not require supplements of meat or vegetables. Dogs do appreciate a little variety in their diets so you may choose to stay with the same brand, but vary the flavour. Alternatively you may wish to add a little flavoured stock to give a difference to the taste.

proprietary puppy food. Selection of the most suitable, good-quality diet at this time is essential, for a puppy's fastest growth rate is during the first year of life. Veterinary surgeons are usually able to offer advice in this regard and, although the frequency of meals will have been reduced over time, only when a young dog has reached the age of about 12 months should an adult diet be fed.

Puppy and junior diets should be well balanced for the needs of your dog, so that except in certain circumstances additional vitamins, minerals and proteins will not be required.

ADULT DIETS
Your Pointer puppy can be put

GRAIN-BASED DIETS

Some less expensive dog foods are based on grains and other plant proteins. While these products may appear to be attractively priced, many breeders prefer a diet based on animal proteins and believe that they are more conducive to your dog's health. Many grain-based diets rely on soy protein that may cause flatulence (passing gas).

There are many cases, however, when your dog might require a special diet. These special require-ments should only be recommended by your veterinary surgeon.

TEST FOR PROPER DIET

A good test for proper diet is the colour, odour and firmness of your dog's stool. A healthy dog usually produces three semi-hard stools per day. The stools should have no unpleasant odour. They should be the same colour from excretion to excretion.

on an adult feeding schedule at around ten to twelve months of age. This means it can be given one main meal a day, preferably at the same time each evening. Most Pointer owners prefer to divide the single meal into two smaller meals given morning and evening.

Meals can be supplemented by a morning or mid-day snack and for this we highly recommend hard dog biscuits made for large dogs. A Pointer has powerful jaws and good strong teeth and can handle those hard biscuits with ease. These not only prove to be a much anticipated treat but do wonders toward maintaining healthy gums and dentition.

There is no simple way to answer the question of what is the best food to give your adult Pointer. We have spoken to successful Pointer breeders in many parts of the world and each breeder we have spoken to seems to have their own tried-and-true method. Probably the

The breeder will have started your Pointer pup on solid food and can give you advice on what to feed. Any changes in diet should be gradually introduced.

What are you feeding your dog?

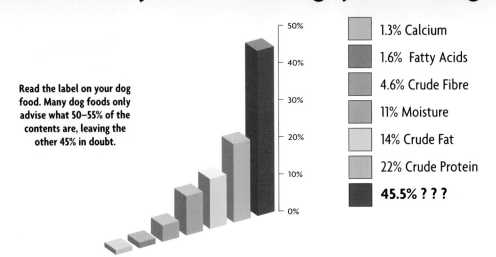

Read the label on your dog food. Many dog foods only advise what 50–55% of the contents are, leaving the other 45% in doubt.

- 1.3% Calcium
- 1.6% Fatty Acids
- 4.6% Crude Fibre
- 11% Moisture
- 14% Crude Fat
- 22% Crude Protein
- **45.5% ? ? ?**

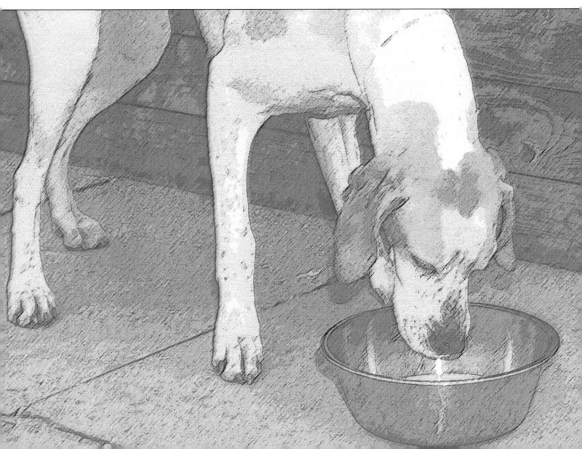

best answer to the question is that you should feed what works best according to weight and general condition. This may not always be what the dog likes best! Who can tell you just what food that is? We sincerely recommend that you consult your veterinary surgeon for his advise in this important matter.

The correct amount of food to maintain a Pointer's optimum condition varies as much from dog to dog as it does from human to human. It is impossible to state any specific amount of food your dog should

DO DOGS HAVE TASTE BUDS?

Watching a dog 'wolf' or gobble his food, seemingly without chewing, leads an owner to wonder whether their dogs can taste anything. Yes, dogs have taste buds, with sensory perception of sweet, salty and sour. Puppies are born with fully mature taste buds.

'DOES THIS COLLAR MAKE ME LOOK FAT?'

While humans may obsess about how they look and how trim their bodies are, many people believe that extra weight on their dogs is a good thing. The truth is, pets should not be over- or under-weight, as both can lead to or signal sickness. In order to tell how fit your pet is, run your hands over his ribs. Are his ribs buried under a layer of fat or are they sticking out considerably? If your pet is within his normal weight range, you should be able to feel the ribs easily. If you stand above him, the outline of his body should resemble an hourglass. Some breeds do tend to be leaner; while some are a bit stockier, but making sure your dog is the right weight for his breed will certainly contribute to his good health.

be given. Much depends upon how much your dog exercises. A Pointer that spends the entire day in the field will need considerably more food than the house dog whose exercise is limited to twenty or thirty minutes of exercise.

Generally speaking, the amount of food for a normally active Pointer is the amount it will eat readily within about 15 minutes of being given the meal. What your dog does not eat in that amount of time should be

FEEDING TIP

Dog food must be at room temperature, neither too hot nor too cold. Fresh water, changed daily and served in a clean bowl, is mandatory, especially when feeding dried food.

Never feed your dog from the table while you are eating. Never feed your dog leftovers from your own meal. They usually contain too much fat and too much seasoning.

Dogs must chew their food. Hard pellets are excellent; soups and slurries are to be avoided.

Don't add left-overs or any extras to normal dog food. The normal food is usually balanced and adding something extra destroys the balance.

Except for age-related changes, dogs do not require dietary variations. They can be fed the same diet, day after day, without their becoming ill.

situation persists and the dog appears to be listless or out of sorts, a visit to the veterinary surgeon is certainly in order.

A good rule of thumb to follow in determining whether or not a Pointer is receiving the proper amount of food is closely monitoring the dog's condition. You should be able to feel the ribs and backbone through a slight layer of muscle and fat.

Dogs, whether they be Pointers or Pekingese, are carnivorous animals, and while the vegetable content of your dog's diet should not be overlooked, a dog's physiology and anatomy are based upon his meat consumption. Protein and fat are absolutely essential in a dog's diet. A great deal of research is conducted by manufacturers of the leading

discarded. Much to the distress of their owners, adolescent Pointers can become temporarily disinterested in food and the thin skin and coats of the breed soon reveal their lack of appetite. Although their owners might think otherwise, dogs will usually eat enough to maintain themselves. This may not appear to be the case by the dog's appearance, but what observers see as being fit and what is actually the case is probably not the same. However, if the

CHANGE IN DIET

As your dog's caretaker, you know the importance of keeping his diet consistent, but sometimes when you run out of food or if you're on holiday, you have to make a change quickly. Some dogs will experience digestive problems but most will not. If you are planning on changing your dog's menu, do so gradually to ensure that your dog will not have any problems. Over a period of four to five days, slowly add some new food to your dog's old food, increasing the percentage of new food each day.

TIPPING THE SCALES

Good nutrition is vital to your dog's health, but many people end up over-feeding or giving unnecessary supplements. Here are some common doggie diet don'ts:

• Adding milk, yoghurt and cheese to your dog's diet may seem like a good idea for coat and skin care, but dairy products are very fattening and can cause indigestion.

• Diets high in fat will not cause heart attacks in dogs but will certainly cause your dog to gain weight.

• Most importantly, don't assume your dog will simply stop eating once he doesn't need any more food. Given the chance, he will eat you out of house and home!

Remember that you can not purchase a top-quality dog food for the same price as one that lacks the nutritional value that you want. In many cases you will find not only does your Pointer need less of the better food, but your dog produces less fecal waste. The highly fortified commercial dog foods seldom require additional vitamin supplementation apart from critical growth periods during puppyhood or in the case of pregnant or lactating females. However, only professionally recommended dosages must be given.

Active dogs like Pointers have higher calorie requirements than more sedentary breeds.

brands of dog food to determine the ideal balance of minerals, protein, carbohydrates and trace elements required for a dog's well-being. Dog food manufacturing has become so sophisticated it is now possible to buy food for dogs living almost any lifestyle from sedentary to highly active.

All dog food brands must list all the ingredients in descending order by weight. The major ingredient is listed first, the next most prominent follows, and so on. Whether canned or dried, look for a food in which the main ingredient is derived from meat, poultry or fish.

LET THE SUN SHINE
Your dog needs daily sunshine for the same reason people do. Pets kept inside homes with curtains drawn against the sun suffer 'SAD' (Seasonal Affected Disorder) to the same degree as humans. We now know that sunlight must enter the iris and thus to the pineal gland to regulate the body's hormonal system and when we live and work in artificial light, both circadian rhythms and hormone balances are disturbed.

SENIOR DIETS

Adult Pointers should be able to remain on a maintenance diet for about eight years. The geriatric or overweight Pointer needs a much lower-calorie diet than the growing puppy or adult dog of normal weight. It is also important to ensure that older dogs get their fair share of exercise each day as even a moderate amount will prolong their life. As dogs get older, their metabolism changes. The older dog usually exercises less, moves more slowly and sleeps more. This change in lifestyle and physiological performance requires a change in diet. Since these changes take place slowly, they might not be recognisable. What is easily recognisable is weight gain. By continuing to feed your dog an adult-maintenance diet when it is slowing down metabolically, your dog will gain weight. Obesity in an older dog compounds the health problems that already accompany old age.

As your dog gets older, few of his organs function up to par. The kidneys slow down and the intestines become less efficient. These age-related factors are best handled with a change in diet and a change in feeding schedule to give smaller portions that are more easily digested.

There is no single best diet for every older dog. While many dogs do well on light or senior diets, other dogs do better on puppy diets or other special premium diets such as lamb and rice. Be sensitive to your senior Pointer's diet and this will help control other problems that may arise with your old friend.

WATER

Just as your dog needs proper nutrition from his food, water is an essential 'nutrient' as well. Water keeps the dog's body properly hydrated and promotes normal function of the body's systems. During housebreaking it is necessary to keep an eye on how much water your Pointer is drinking, but once he is reliably trained he should have access to clean fresh water at all times, especially if you feed dried food. Make certain that the dog's water bowl is clean, and change the water often.

EXERCISE

Food, water and exercise: it is impossible to have a happy healthy Pointer without sufficient amounts of each. The bored inactive Pointer would be extremely unhappy and more than capable of wreaking havoc in a confining environment.

The family Pointer can make an ideal jogging companion, an enthusiastic agility and obedience candidate and an excellent field trial dog. It is the

DRINK, DRANK, DRUNK— MAKE IT A DOUBLE

In both humans and dogs, as well as most living organisms, water forms the major part of nearly every body tissue. Naturally, we take water for granted, but without it, life as we know it would cease.

For dogs, water is needed to keep their bodies functioning biochemically. Additionally, water is needed to replace the water lost while panting. Unlike humans who are able to sweat to dissipate heat, dogs must pant to cool down, thereby losing the vital water from their bodies needed to regulate their body temperatures. Humans lose electrolyte-containing products and other body-fluid components through sweating; dogs do not lose anything except water.

Water is essential always, but especially so when the weather is hot or humid or when your dog is exercising or working vigorously.

should never be subjected to an intense jogging programme before it has reached full maturity.

For the Pointer's sanity (as well as that of his owner), daily exercise is the key to happiness. Any active mind is a balanced mind, especially where the Pointer is concerned. The Pointer is, by and large, one of the most active dogs any owner could choose and therefore requires considerable outdoor attention. Do not give your Pointer the opportunity to hone his destructive skills—give him plenty of activity, in the garden, on the field, on the beach, etc.

GROOMING
Your Pointer will not demand much of your time or equipment in the way of grooming but the dog still requires care. Regular brushing sessions keep the coat clean, odour-free and healthy. This gives the groomer an opportunity to be aware of and treat any skin problems that might arise.

Pointers will cast their coats twice a year. Brushing is an absolute necessity at this time. Even though the Pointer's coat is short, you will be amazed at the amount of hair deposited throughout the house if a regular brushing regimen is not followed.

owner's decision. Puppies should never be forced to exercise. Normally, Pointer puppies are little dynamos of energy and keep themselves busy all day long, interspersed with frequent naps. A Pointer

Regular grooming also gives you the opportunity to respond immediately to your dog's health care needs. Such things as clipping nails, cleaning ears and checking teeth can be taken care of during the time set aside for grooming.

Investing in a grooming table that has a non-slip top, and an arm and a noose can make all of these activities infinitely easier. These tables are available at pet shops and it is important to choose a table with a height that allows you to stand or sit comfortably while you are working on your dog. A grooming table that has an arm and a noose keeps the dog from fidgeting or deciding it has had enough grooming.

GROOMING EQUIPMENT

How much grooming equipment you purchase will depend on how much grooming you are going to do. Here are some basics:

- Stiff bristle brush
- Grooming table
- Steel comb
- Scissors
- Blaster
- Rubber mat
- Dog shampoo
- Spray hose attachment
- Ear cleaner
- Cotton wipes
- Towels
- Nail clippers

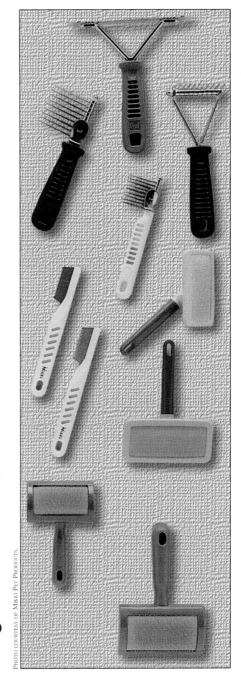

You really don't need many grooming tools for your Pointer, but a basic comb and brush will help remove dead hairs and keep your Pointer's smooth coat in top condition.

PHOTO COURTESY OF MIKKI PET PRODUCTS.

trimmed and having its feet inspected. Check between the toes for splinters and thorns, paying particular attention to any swollen or tender areas.

In some sections of the country there is a weed called the fox-tail that has a barbed hook-like structure that carries its seed. This hook easily finds its way into a dog's foot or between its toes and very quickly works its way deep into the dog's flesh, causing soreness and infection. These barbs are best removed by your veterinary surgeon before serious problems arise.

BATHING

Dogs do not need to be bathed as often as humans, but regular bathing is essential for healthy skin and a healthy, shiny coat. Again, like most anything, if you accustom your pup to being bathed as a puppy, it will be second nature by the time he grows up. You want your dog to be at ease in the bath or else it could end up a wet, soapy, messy ordeal for both of you!

Brush your Pointer thoroughly before wetting his coat. This will get rid of most mats and tangles, which are harder to remove when the coat is wet. Make certain that your dog has a good non-slip surface to stand on. Begin by wetting the dog's coat. A shower or hose

A hound glove can be used to put the finishing touches on your Pointer's coat and give it extra shine. Many dogs actually like the feeling of being brushed with a glove.

Invest in a good stiff bristle brush, a steel comb and animal nail clippers or a drummel that grinds the nails down rather than actually cutting them. You will be using this equipment for many years so buy the best equipment you can afford.

The Pointer is a natural breed with a coat that requires no clipping or trimming. This is a good time to accustom your Pointer to having its nails attachment is necessary for thoroughly wetting and rinsing the coat. Check the water temperature to make sure that it is neither too hot nor too cold.

Next, apply shampoo to the dog's coat and work it into a good lather. You should purchase a shampoo that is made for dogs. Do not use a product made for human hair. Wash the head last; you do not want shampoo to drip into the dog's eyes while you are washing the rest of his body. Work the shampoo all the way down to the skin. You can use this opportunity to check the skin for any bumps, bites or other abnormalities. Do not neglect any area of the body—get all of the hard-to-reach places.

Once the dog has been thoroughly shampooed, he requires an equally thorough rinsing. Shampoo left in the coat

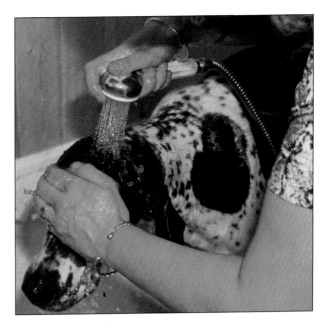

can be irritating to the skin. Protect his eyes from the shampoo by shielding them with your hand and directing the flow of water in the opposite direction. You should also avoid getting water in the ear canal. Be prepared for your dog to shake out his coat—you might want to stand back, but make sure you have a hold on the dog to keep him from running through the house.

Shield your Pointer's eyes when wetting his head. Also pay attention to not spraying water into the ears.

EAR CLEANING
The ears should be kept clean with a cotton wipe and ear powder made especially for dogs. Be on the lookout for any signs of infection or ear mite infestation. If your Pointer has been shaking his head or

SOAP IT UP
The use of human soap products like shampoo, bubble bath and hand soap can be damaging to a dog's coat and skin. Human products are too strong and remove the protective oils coating the dog's hair and skin (making him water-resistant). Use only shampoo made especially for dogs and you may like to use a medicated shampoo, which will always help to keep external parasites at bay.

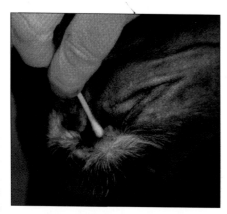

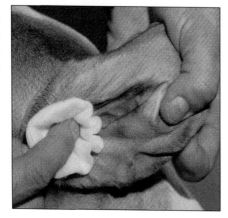

Do not forget to clean your Pointer's ears! Ask your veterinary surgeon to show you how to do it. Rather than probing with a cotton bud (top), use a cotton wipe (bottom) made especially for the task.

or on grass when outdoors can grow long very quickly. Do not allow the nails to become overgrown and then expect to cut them back easily.

Each nail has a blood vessel running through the centre called the 'quick.' The quick grows close to the end of the nail and contains very sensitive nerve endings. If the nail is allowed to grow too long, it will be impossible to cut it back to a proper length without cutting into the quick. This is very painful and can also result in profuse bleeding that can be very difficult to stop.

If your Pointer is getting plenty of exercise on cement or rough hard pavement, the nails may stay sufficiently worn down; otherwise, the nails can grow long. They must then be trimmed with canine nail clippers, an electric nail grinder or a coarse file made expressly for that purpose. Regardless of which nail trimming device is used, you must proceed with caution and remove only a small portion of the nail at a time.

Should the quick be nipped in the trimming process, there are any number of blood-clotting products available at pet shops that will almost immediately stem the flow of blood. It is wise to have one of these products on hand in case your dog breaks a nail in some way.

scratching at his ears frequently, this usually indicates a problem. If his ears have an unusual odour, this is a sure sign of mite infestation or infection, and a signal to have his ears checked by the veterinary surgeon.

NAIL CLIPPING

We suggest attending to your dog's nails every other week. The nails of a Pointer that spends most of its time indoors

TRAVELLING WITH YOUR DOG

CAR TRAVEL

You should accustom your Pointer to riding in a car at an early age. You may or may not take him in the car often, but at the very least he will need to go to the vet and you do not want these trips to be traumatic for the dog or troublesome for you.

PEDICURE TIP

A dog that spends a lot of time outside on a hard surface, such as cement or pavement, will have his nails naturally worn down and may not need to have them trimmed as often, except maybe in the colder months when he is not outside as much. Regardless, it is best to get your dog accustomed to this procedure at an early age so that he is used to it. Some dogs are especially sensitive about having their feet touched, but if a dog has experienced it since he was young, he should not be bothered by it.

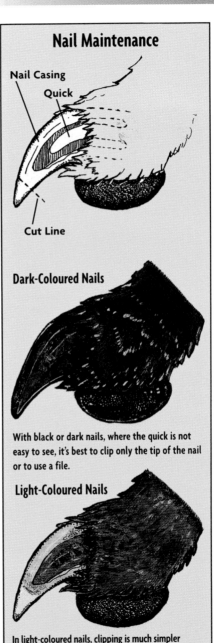

Nail Maintenance

Nail Casing

Quick

Cut Line

Dark-Coloured Nails

With black or dark nails, where the quick is not easy to see, it's best to clip only the tip of the nail or to use a file.

Light-Coloured Nails

In light-coloured nails, clipping is much simpler because you can see the vein (or quick) that grows inside the casing.

Clipping or grinding down your Pointer's nails is a must unless the dog spends a lot of time walking on hard surfaces.

Clip only the bottom portion of the nail, avoiding the quick. If you cut into the quick, the nail will bleed and the dog will experience pain. A styptic pencil will stop the bleeding. Reassure the injured dog by talking quietly to him.

Use a soft wipe to gently clean the area around your Pointer's eyes.

If you are going on a long motor trip with your dog, be sure the hotels are dog friendly. Many hotels do not accept dogs. Also take along some ice that can be thawed and offered to your dog if he becomes overheated. Most dogs like to lick ice.

the vehicle—this is very dangerous! If you should stop short, your dog can be thrown and injured. If the dog starts climbing on you and pestering you while you are driving, you will not be able to concentrate on the road. It is an unsafe situation for everyone—human and canine.

For long trips, be prepared to stop to let the dog relieve himself. Take with you whatever

The safest way for a dog to ride in the car is in his crate. If he uses a crate in the house, you can use the same crate for travel, provided that your vehicle can accommodate it.

Put the pup in the crate and see how he reacts. If he seems uneasy, you can have a passenger hold him on his lap while you drive. Another option is a specially made safety harness for dogs, which straps the dog in much like a seat belt. Do not let the dog roam loose in

MOTION SICKNESS

*If life is a motorway...*your dog may not want to come along for the ride! Some dogs experience motion sickness in cars that leads to excessive salivation and even vomiting. In most cases, your dog will fare better in the familiar, safe confines of his crate. To desensitise your dog, try going on several short jaunts before trying a long trip. If your dog experiences distress when riding in the vehicle, drive with him only when absolutely necessary, and do not feed him or give him water before you go.

you need to clean up after him, including some paper kitchen towels and perhaps some old towelling for use should he have an accident in the car or suffer from travel sickness.

AIR TRAVEL

While it is possible to take a dog on a flight within Britain, this is fairly unusual and advance permission is always required. The dog will be required to travel in a fibreglass crate and you should always check in advance with the airline regarding specific requirements. To help the dog be at ease, put one of his favourite toys in the crate with him. Do not feed the dog for at least six hours before the trip to minimise his need to relieve himself. However, certain regulations specify that water must always be made available to the dog in the crate.

Make sure your dog is properly identified and that your contact information appears on

his ID tags and on his crate. Animals travel in a different area of the plane than human passengers so every rule must be strictly adhered to so as to prevent the risk of getting separated from your dog.

BOARDING

So you want to take a family holiday—and you want to include *all* members of the family. You would probably make arrangements for accommodation ahead of time anyway, but this is especially important when travelling with a dog. You do not want to make an overnight stop at the only place around for miles and find out that they do not allow dogs.

If you are going on holiday and need to board your Pointer, research boarding kennels ahead of time. Select a clean kennel with an attentive staff and enough room to allow your Pointer his required daily exercise.

Also, you do not want to reserve a place for your family without confirming that you are travelling with a dog because if it is against their policy you may not have a place to stay.

Alternatively, if you are travelling and choose not to bring your Pointer, you will have to make arrangements for him while you are away. Some options are to take him to a neighbour's house to stay while you are gone, to have a trusted neighbour pop in often or stay at your house, or bring your dog to a reputable boarding kennel. If you choose to board him at a kennel, you should visit in advance to see the facilities provided, how clean they are and where the dogs are kept. Talk to some of the employees and see how they treat the dogs—do they spend time with

ABUSING YOUR BEST FRIEND

As an educated and caring pet owner, you may believe that everyone wants to invest countless hours (and pounds) in order to raise a loving and well-adjusted canine companion. Sadly, this is not the case, as dogs account for almost half of all victims of animal abuse. Remember, abuse implies not only beating or torturing an animal but also neglecting the animal, such as failing to provide adequate shelter and food or emotional fulfilment.

the dogs, play with them, exercise them, etc.? Also find out the kennel's policy on vaccinations and what they require. This is for all of the dogs' safety, since when dogs are kept together, there is a greater risk of diseases being passed from dog to dog.

IDENTIFICATION

Your Pointer is your valued companion and friend. That is why you always keep a close eye on him and you have made sure that he cannot escape from the garden or wriggle out of his collar and run away from you. However, accidents can happen and there may come a time

when your dog unexpectedly gets separated from you. If this unfortunate event should occur, the first thing on your mind will be finding him. Proper identification, including an ID tag, a tattoo, and possibly a microchip, will increase the chances of his being returned to you safely and quickly.

IDENTITY CRISIS!

Surely you know the importance of good nutrition, good training and a good home, but are you aware of the importance of identification tags for your dog? If your dog ran away or got lost, ID tags on your pet's collar would provide crucial information such as the dog's name, the owner's name and address, making it possible that your dog would soon be returned. Every morning before taking your dog out, make sure his collar and tags are present and securely fastened.

Housebreaking and Training Your
POINTER

REAP THE REWARDS

If you start with a normal, healthy dog and give him time, patience and some carefully executed lessons, you will reap the rewards of that training for the life of the dog. And what a life it will be! The two of you will find immeasurable pleasure in the companionship you have built together with love, respect and understanding.

Living with an untrained dog is a lot like owning a piano that you do not know how to play—it is a nice object to look at but it does not do much more than that to bring you pleasure. Now try taking piano lessons and suddenly the piano comes alive and brings forth magical sounds and rhythms that set your heart singing and your body swaying.

The same is true with your Pointer. Any dog is a big responsibility and if not trained sensibly may develop unacceptable behaviour that annoys you or could even cause family friction.

To train your Pointer, you may like to enrol in an obedience class. Teach him good manners as you learn how and why he behaves the way he does. Find out how to communicate with your dog and how to recognise and understand his communications with you. Suddenly the dog takes on a new role in your life—he is clever, interesting, well-behaved and fun to be with. He demonstrates his bond of devotion to you daily. In other words, your Pointer does wonders for your ego because he constantly reminds you that you are not only his leader, you are his hero!

Those involved with teaching dog obedience and counselling owners about their dogs' behaviour have discovered some interesting facts about dog ownership. For example, training dogs when they are puppies results in the highest rate of success in developing well-mannered and well-adjusted adult dogs. Training an older dog, from six months to six years of age, can produce almost equal results providing that the owner accepts the dog's slower rate of learning capability and is willing to work patiently to help the dog succeed at developing to his fullest potential. Unfortunately, many owners of untrained adult dogs lack the patience factor, so they do not persist until their dogs are successful at learning particular

behaviours.

Training a puppy aged 10 to 16 weeks (20 weeks at the most) is like working with a dry sponge in a pool of water. The pup soaks up whatever you show him and constantly looks for more things to do and learn. At this early age, his body is not yet producing hormones, and therein lies the reason for such a high rate of success. Without hormones, he is focused on his owners and not particularly interested in investigating other places, dogs, people, etc. You are his leader: his provider of food, water, shelter and security. He latches onto you and wants to stay close. He will usually follow you from room to room, will not let you out of his sight when you are outdoors with him and will respond in like manner

The Pointer's instinctive traits must be taken into account when undertaking training.

PARENTAL GUIDANCE

Training a dog is a life experience. Many parents admit that much of what they know about raising children they learned from caring for their dogs. Dogs respond to love, fairness and guidance, just as children do. Become a good dog owner and you may become an even better parent.

THINK BEFORE YOU BARK

Dogs are sensitive to their master's moods and emotions. Use your voice wisely when communicating with your dog. Never raise your voice at your dog unless you are angry and trying to correct him. 'Barking' at your dog can become as meaningless as 'dogspeak' is to you. Think before you bark!

him. It is at this time when you may notice that the untrained dog begins to wander away from you and even ignore your commands to stay close. When this behaviour becomes a problem, the owner has two choices: get rid of the dog or train him. It is strongly urged that you choose the latter option.

There are usually classes within a reasonable distance from the owner's home, but you can also do a lot to train your dog yourself. Sometimes there are classes available but the tuition is too costly. Whatever the circumstances, the solution to the problem of lack of lesson availability lies within the pages of this book.

This chapter is devoted to helping you train your Pointer at home. If the recommended procedures are followed faithfully, you may expect positive results that will prove rewarding both to you and your dog.

to the people and animals you encounter. If you greet a friend warmly, he will be happy to greet the person as well. If, however, you are hesitant, even anxious, about the approach of a stranger, he will respond accordingly.

Once the puppy begins to produce hormones, his natural curiosity emerges and he begins to investigate the world around

HONOUR AND OBEY

Dogs are the most honourable animals in existence. They consider another species (humans) as their own. They interface with you. You are their leader. Puppies perceive children to be on their level; their actions around small children are different from their behaviour around their adult masters.

Whether your new charge is a puppy or a mature adult, the methods of teaching and the techniques we use in training basic behaviours are the same. After all, no dog, whether puppy or adult, likes harsh or inhumane methods. All creatures, however, respond favourably to gentle motivational methods and sincere praise and encouragement. Now let us get started.

HOUSEBREAKING

You can train a puppy to relieve itself wherever you choose, but this must be somewhere suitable. You should bear in mind from the outset that when your puppy is old enough to go out in public places, any canine deposits must be removed at once. You will always have to carry with you a small plastic bag or 'poop-scoop.'

Outdoor training includes such surfaces as grass, soil and cement. Indoor training usually

means training your dog to newspaper.

When deciding on the surface and location that you will want your Pointer to use, be sure it is going to be permanent. Training your dog to grass and then changing your mind two months later is extremely difficult for both dog and owner.

Next, choose the command you will use each and every time you want your puppy to void. 'Hurry up' and 'Be quick' are examples of commands commonly used by dog owners.

Get in the habit of giving the puppy your chosen relief command before you take him out. That way, when he becomes an adult, you will be able to determine if he wants to go out when you ask him. A confirmation will be signs of interest, wagging his tail, watching you intently, going to the door, etc.

You select the area in which your Pointer is to relieve himself. Once trained, he will always return to the same spot.

THE HAND THAT FEEDS

To a dog's way of thinking, your hands are like his mouth in terms of a defence mechanism. If you squeeze him too tightly, he might just bite you because that would be his normal response. This is not aggressive biting and, although all biting should be discouraged, you need the discipline in learning how to handle your dog.

93

immediately after sleeping and eating. The older the puppy, the less often he will need to relieve himself. Finally, as a mature healthy adult, he will require only three to five relief trips per day.

HOUSING
Since the types of housing and control you provide for your puppy have a direct relationship on the success of housetraining, we consider the various aspects of both before we begin training.

Taking a new puppy home and turning him loose in your house can be compared to turning a child loose in a sports arena and telling the child that the place is all his! The sheer enormity of the place would be too much for him to handle.

Instead, offer the puppy

Once housebroken, your Pointer will let you know when he needs to 'go out.' Learn to recognise the signs.

PUPPY'S NEEDS
Puppy needs to relieve himself after play periods, after each meal, after he has been sleeping and at any time he indicates that he is looking for a place to urinate or defecate.

The urinary and intestinal tract muscles of very young puppies are not fully developed. Therefore, like human babies, puppies need to relieve themselves frequently.

Take your puppy out often—every hour for an eight-week-old, for example, and always

PAPER CAPER
Never line your pup's sleeping area with newspaper. Puppy litters are usually raised on newspaper and, once in your home, the puppy will immediately associate newspaper with voiding. Never put newspaper on any floor while housetraining, as this will only confuse the puppy. If you are paper-training him, use paper in his designated relief area ONLY. Finally, restrict water intake after evening meals. Offer a few licks at a time—never let a young puppy gulp water after meals.

clearly defined areas where he can play, sleep, eat and live. A room of the house where the family gathers is the most obvious choice. Puppies are social animals and need to feel a part of the pack right from the start. Hearing your voice, watching you while you are doing things and smelling you nearby are all positive reinforcers that he is now a member of your pack. Usually the sitting room, the kitchen or a nearby adjoining breakfast area is ideal for providing safety and security for both puppy and owner.

Within that room there should be a smaller area that the puppy can call his own. An alcove, a wire or fibreglass dog crate or a fenced (not boarded!) corner from which he can view the activities of his new family will be fine. The size of the area or crate is the key factor here. The area must be large enough for the puppy to lie down and stretch out as well as stand up without rubbing his head on the top, yet small enough so that he cannot relieve himself at one end and sleep at the other without coming into contact with his droppings. This will be the situation until he is fully trained to relieve himself outside.

Dogs are, by nature, clean animals and will not remain

GETTING YOUR ATTENTION

Dogs will do anything for your attention. If you reward the dog when he is calm and resting, you will develop a well-mannered dog. If, on the other hand, you greet your dog excitedly and encourage him to wrestle with you, the dog will greet you the same way and you will have a hyperactive dog on your hands.

95

ATTENTION!
Your dog is actually training you at the same time you are training him. Dogs do things to get attention. They usually repeat whatever succeeds in getting your attention.

close to their relief areas unless forced to do so. In those cases, they then become dirty dogs and usually remain that way for life.

The designated area should contain clean bedding and a toy. Water must always be available, in a non-spill container.

Control

By control, we mean helping the puppy to create a lifestyle pattern that will be compatible to that of his human pack (YOU!). Just as we guide little children to learn our way of life, we must show the puppy when it is time to play, eat, sleep, exercise and even entertain himself.

Your puppy should always sleep in his crate. He should also learn that, during times of household confusion and excessive human activity such as at breakfast when family members are preparing for the day, he can play by himself in relative safety and comfort in his designated area. Each time you leave the puppy alone, he should understand exactly where he is to stay. Puppies are chewers. They cannot tell the difference between lamp cords, television wires, shoes, table legs, etc. Chewing into a television wire, for example, can be fatal to the puppy while a shorted wire can start a fire in the house.

If the puppy chews on the arm of the chair when he is alone, you will probably discipline him angrily when you get home. Thus, he makes the association that your coming home means he is going to be punished. (He will not remember chewing the chair and is incapable of making the association of the discipline with his naughty deed.)

Other times of excitement, such as family parties, etc., can be fun for the puppy providing he can view the activities from the security of his designated area. He is not underfoot and he is not being fed all sorts of titbits that will probably cause him

CANINE DEVELOPMENT SCHEDULE

It is important to understand how and at what age a puppy develops into adulthood. If you are a puppy owner, consult the following Canine Development Schedule to determine the stage of development your puppy is currently experiencing. This knowledge will help you as you work with the puppy in the weeks and months ahead.

Period	Age	Characteristics
FIRST TO THIRD	BIRTH TO SEVEN WEEKS	Puppy needs food, sleep and warmth, and responds to simple and gentle touching. Needs mother for security and disciplining. Needs littermates for learning and interacting with other dogs. Pup learns to function within a pack and learns pack order of dominance. Begin socialising with adults and children for short periods. Begins to become aware of its environment.
FOURTH	EIGHT TO TWELVE WEEKS	Brain is fully developed. Needs socialising with outside world. Remove from mother and littermates. Needs to change from canine pack to human pack. Human dominance necessary. Fear period occurs between 8 and 16 weeks. Avoid fright and pain.
FIFTH	THIRTEEN TO SIXTEEN WEEKS	Training and formal obedience should begin. Less association with other dogs, more with people, places, situations. Period will pass easily if you remember this is pup's change-to-adolescence time. Be firm and fair. Flight instinct prominent. Permissiveness and over-disciplining can do permanent damage. Praise for good behaviour.
JUVENILE	FOUR TO EIGHT MONTHS	Another fear period about 7 to 8 months of age. It passes quickly, but be cautious of fright and pain. Sexual maturity reached. Dominant traits established. Dog should understand sit, down, come and stay by now.

NOTE: THESE ARE APPROXIMATE TIME FRAMES. ALLOW FOR INDIVIDUAL DIFFERENCES IN PUPPIES.

A crate is the most valuable training tool you can buy. Your puppy will come to think of it as his own special place.

HOW MANY TIMES A DAY?

AGE	RELIEF TRIPS
To 14 weeks	10
14–22 weeks	8
22–32 weeks	6
Adulthood	4
(dog stops growing)	

These are estimates, of course, but they are a guide to the MINIMUM opportunities a dog should have each day to relieve itself.

stomach distress, yet he still feels a part of the fun.

SCHEDULE

A puppy should be taken to his relief area each time he is released from his designated area, after meals, after a play session and when he first awakens in the morning (at age eight weeks, this can mean 5 a.m.!). The puppy will indicate that he's ready 'to go' by circling or sniffing busily—do not misinterpret these signs. For a puppy less than ten weeks of age, a routine of taking him out every hour is necessary. As the puppy grows, he will be able to wait for longer periods of time.

Keep trips to his relief area short. Stay no more than five or six minutes and then return to the house. If he goes during that time, praise him lavishly and take him indoors immediately. If he does not, but he has an accident when you go back indoors, pick him up immedi-ately, say 'No! No!' and return to his relief area. Wait a few minutes, then return to the

house again. Never hit a puppy or rub his face in urine or excrement when he has had an accident!

Once indoors, put the puppy in his crate until you have had time to clean up his accident. Then release him to the family area and watch him more closely than before. Chances are, his accident was a result of your not picking up his signal or waiting too long before offering him the

MEALTIME

Mealtime should be a peaceful time for your puppy. Do not put his food and water bowls in a high-traffic area in the house. For example, give him his own little corner of the kitchen where he can eat undisturbed and where he will not be underfoot. Do not allow small children or other family members to disturb the pup when he is eating.

Kinnike Lynda, shown at four weeks of age. Very young puppies need to relieve themselves often and have little control. Their control, of course, improves with age and training.

TAKE THE LEAD

Do not carry your dog to his toilet area. Lead him there on a leash or, better yet, encourage him to follow you to the spot. If you start carrying him to his spot, you might end up doing this routine forever and your dog will have the satisfaction of having trained YOU.

opportunity to relieve himself. Never hold a grudge against the puppy for accidents.

Let the puppy learn that going outdoors means it is time to relieve himself, not play. Once trained, he will be able to play indoors and out and still differentiate between the times for play versus the times for relief.

Help him develop regular hours for naps, being alone, playing by himself and just resting, all in his crate. Encourage him to entertain himself while you are busy with your activities. Let him learn that having you near is comforting, but it is not your main purpose in life to provide him with undivided attention.

Each time you put a puppy in his own area, use the same command, whatever suits best. Soon he will run to his crate or special area when he hears you say those words.

Crate training provides safety for you, the puppy and the home. It also provides the puppy with a feeling of security, and that helps the puppy achieve self-confidence and clean habits.

Remember that one of the primary ingredients in housetraining your puppy is control. Regardless of your lifestyle, there will always be occasions when you will need to

THE GOLDEN RULE

The golden rule of dog training is simple. For each 'question' (command), there is only one correct answer (reaction). One command = one reaction. Keep practising the command until the dog reacts correctly without hesitating. Be repetitive but not monotonous. Dogs get bored just as people do!

have a place where your dog can stay and be happy and safe. Crate training is the answer for now and in the future.

In conclusion, a few key elements are really all you need for a successful house training method—consistency, frequency, praise, control and supervision. By following these procedures with a normal, healthy puppy, you and the puppy will soon be past the stage of 'accidents' and ready to move on to a full and rewarding life together.

ROLES OF DISCIPLINE, REWARD AND PUNISHMENT

Discipline, training one to act in accordance with rules, brings order to life. It is as simple as that. Without discipline, particularly in a group society, chaos reigns supreme and the group will eventually perish. Humans and canines are social animals and need some form of discipline in order to function effectively. They must procure food, protect their home base and their young and reproduce to keep the species going.

THE SUCCESS METHOD

1 Tell the puppy 'Crate time!' and place him in the crate with a small treat (a piece of cheese or half of a biscuit). Let him stay in the crate for five minutes while you are in the same room. Then release him and praise lavishly. Never release him when he is fussing. Wait until he is quiet before you let him out.

2 Repeat Step 1 several times a day.

3 The next day, place the puppy in the crate as before. Let him stay there for ten minutes. Do this several times.

4 Continue building time in five-minute increments until the puppy

stays in his crate for 30 minutes with you in the room. Always take him to his relief area after prolonged periods in his crate.

5 Now go back to Step 1 and let the puppy stay in his crate for five minutes, this time while you are out of the room.

6 Once again, build crate time in five-minute increments with you out of the room. When the puppy will stay willingly in his crate (he may even fall asleep!) for 30 minutes with you out of the room, he will be ready to stay in it for several hours at a time.

6 Steps to Successful Crate Training

THE SUCCESS METHOD

Success that comes by luck is usually short lived. Success that comes by well-thought-out proven methods is often more easily achieved and permanent. This is the Success Method. It is designed to give you, the puppy owner, a simple yet proven way to help your puppy develop clean living habits and a feeling of security in his new environment.

THE CLEAN LIFE

By providing sleeping and resting quarters that fit the dog, and offering frequent opportunities to relieve himself outside his quarters, the puppy quickly learns that the outdoors (or the newspaper if you are training him to paper) is the place to go when he needs to urinate or defecate. It also reinforces his innate desire to keep his sleeping quarters clean. This, in turn, helps develop the muscle control that will eventually produce a dog with clean living habits.

If there were no discipline in the lives of social animals, they would eventually die from starvation and/or predation by other stronger animals.

In the case of domestic canines, dogs need discipline in their lives in order to understand how their pack (you and other family members) functions and how they must act in order to survive.

A large humane society in a highly populated area recently surveyed dog owners regarding their satisfaction with their relationships with their dogs. People who had trained their dogs were 75% more satisfied with their pets than those who had never trained their dogs.

Dr Edward Thorndike, a psychologist, established *Thorndike's Theory of Learning*, which states that a behaviour that results in a pleasant event tends to be repeated. A behaviour that results in an unpleasant event tends not to be repeated. It is this theory on which training methods are based today. For example, if you manipulate a dog to perform a specific behaviour and reward him for doing it, he is likely to

101

Always clean up after your dog.

told many times to leave the cat alone, yet he persists in teasing the cat. Then, one day he begins chasing the cat but the cat turns and swipes a claw across the dog's face, leaving him with a painful gash on his nose. The final result is that the dog stops chasing the cat.

do it again because he enjoyed the end result.

Occasionally, punishment, a penalty inflicted for an offence, is necessary. The best type of punishment often comes from an outside source. For example, a child is told not to touch the stove because he may get burned. He disobeys and touches the stove. In doing so, he receives a burn. From that time on, he respects the heat of the stove and avoids contact with it. Therefore, a behaviour that results in an unpleasant event tends not to be repeated.

A good example of a dog learning the hard way is the dog who chases the house cat. He is

COMMAND STANCE

Stand up straight and authoritatively when giving your dog commands. Do not issue commands when lying on the floor or lying on your back on the sofa. If you are on your hands and knees when you give a command, your dog will think you are positioning yourself to play.

TRAINING EQUIPMENT

COLLAR AND LEAD

For a Pointer the collar and lead that you use for training must be one with which you are easily able to work, not too heavy for the dog and perfectly safe.

TREATS

Have a bag of treats on hand. Something nutritious and easy to swallow works best. Use a soft treat, a chunk of cheese or a piece of cooked chicken rather than a dry biscuit. By the time the dog has finished chewing a dry treat, he will forget why he is being rewarded in the first

Always introduce new lessons with the dog on lead. Here, a Pointer and his owner practise the sit/stay.

place! Using food rewards will not teach a dog to beg at the table—the only way to teach a dog to beg at the table is to give him food from the table. In training, rewarding the dog with a food treat will help him associate praise and the treats with learning new behaviours that obviously please his owner.

TRAINING BEGINS: ASK THE DOG A QUESTION

In order to teach your dog anything, you must first get his attention. After all, he cannot learn anything if he is looking away from you with his mind on something else.

To get his attention, ask him, 'School?' and immediately walk over to him and give him a treat as you tell him 'Good dog.' Wait a minute or two and repeat the routine, this time with a treat in your hand as you approach within a foot of the dog. Do not go directly to him, but stop about a foot short of him and hold out the treat as you ask, 'School?' He will see you approaching with a treat in your hand and most likely begin walking toward you. As you meet, give him the treat and praise again.

The third time, ask the question, have a treat in your hand and walk only a short distance toward the dog so that he must walk almost all the way

PRACTICE MAKES PERFECT!

- Have training lessons with your dog every day in several short segments—three to five times a day for a few minutes at a time is ideal.
- Do not have long practice sessions. The dog will become easily bored.
- Never practise when you are tired, ill, worried or in an otherwise negative mood. This will transmit to the dog and may have an adverse effect on its performance.

Think fun, short and above all POSITIVE! End each session on a high note, rather than a failed exercise, and make sure to give a lot of praise. Enjoy the training and help your dog enjoy it, too.

to you. As he reaches you, give him the treat and praise again.

By this time, the dog will probably be getting the idea that if he pays attention to you, especially when you ask that question, it will pay off in treats and enjoyable activities for him. In other words, he learns that 'school' means doing great things with you that are fun and result in positive attention for him.

Remember that the dog does not understand your verbal language; he only recognises sounds. Your question translates to a series of sounds for him, and those sounds become the signal to go to you and pay attention; if he does, he will get to interact with you plus receive treats and praise.

THE BASIC COMMANDS

TEACHING SIT
Now that you have the dog's attention, attach his lead and hold it in your left hand and a food treat in your right. Place your food hand at the dog's nose and let him lick the treat but not take it from you. Say 'Sit' and slowly raise your food hand from in front of the dog's nose up over his head so that he is looking at the ceiling. As he bends his head upward, he will have to bend his knees to maintain his balance. As he

bends his knees, he will assume a sit position. At that point, release the food treat and praise lavishly with comments such as 'Good dog! Good sit!,' etc. Remember to always praise enthusiastically, because dogs relish verbal praise from their owners and feel so proud of themselves whenever they accomplish a behaviour.

You will not use food forever in getting the dog to obey your commands. Food is only used to teach new behaviours, and once the dog knows what you want when you give a specific command, you will wean him off the food treats but still maintain the verbal praise. After all, you will always have your voice with you, and there will be many times when you have no food rewards but expect the dog to obey.

TEACHING DOWN
Teaching the down exercise is easy when you understand how the dog perceives the down position, and it is very difficult when you do not. Dogs perceive the down position as a submissive one, therefore teaching the down exercise using a forceful method can sometimes make the dog develop such a fear of the down that he either runs away when you say 'Down' or he attempts to snap at the person who tries to force him down.

Teaching the sit is the most basic command and the first you will teach your Pointer. Sometimes you may have to guide the dog into the proper position until he is familiar with it.

THE STUDENT'S STRESS TEST

During training sessions you must be able to recognise signs of stress in your dog such as:

- tucking his tail between his legs
- lowering his head
- shivering or trembling
- standing completely still or running away
- panting and/or salivating
- avoiding eye contact
- flattening his ears back
- urinating submissively
- rolling over and lifting a leg
- grinning or baring teeth
- aggression when restrained

If your four-legged student displays these signs he may just be nervous or intimidated. The training session may have been too lengthy with not enough praise and affirmation. Stop for the day and try again tomorrow.

Have the dog sit close alongside your left leg, facing in the same direction as you are. Hold the lead in your left hand and a food treat in your right. Now place your left hand lightly on the top of the dog's shoulders where they meet above the spinal cord. Do not push down on the dog's shoulders; simply rest your left hand there so you can guide the dog to lie down close to your left leg rather than to swing away from your side when he drops.

Now place the food hand at the dog's nose, say 'Down' very softly (almost a whisper), and slowly lower the food hand to the dog's front feet. When the food hand reaches the floor, begin moving it forward along the floor in front of the dog. Keep talking softly to the dog, saying things like, 'Do you want this treat? You can do this, good dog.' Your reassuring tone of voice will help calm the dog as he tries to follow the food hand in order to get the treat.

When the dog's elbows touch the floor, release the food and praise softly. Try to get the dog to maintain that down position for several seconds before you let him sit up again. The goal here is to get the dog to settle down and not feel threatened in the down position.

TEACHING STAY

It is easy to teach the dog to stay in either a sit or a down

DOUBLE JEOPARDY

A dog in jeopardy never lies down. He stays alert on his feet because instinct tells him that he may have to run away or fight for his survival. Therefore, if a dog feels threatened or anxious, he will not lie down. Consequently, it is important to have the dog calm and relaxed as he learns the down exercise.

position. Again, we use food and praise during the teaching process as we help the dog to understand exactly what it is that we are expecting him to do.

To teach the sit/stay, start with the dog sitting on your left side as before and hold the lead in your left hand. Have a food treat in your right hand and place your food hand at the dog's nose. Say 'Stay' and step out on your right foot to stand directly in front of the dog, toe to toe, as he licks and nibbles the treat. Be sure to keep his head facing upward to maintain the sit position. Count to five and then swing around to stand next to the dog again with him on your left. As soon as you get back to the original position, release the food and praise lavishly.

Top: Guiding the dog from the sit position to the down position. Bottom: Practice makes perfect! The dog is comfortable with the down position and assumes it on his own.

'NO' MEANS 'NO!'

Dogs do not understand our language. They can be trained to react to a certain sound, at a certain volume. If you say 'No, Oliver' in a very soft pleasant voice it will not have the same meaning as 'No, Oliver!!' when you shout it as loud as you can. You should never use the dog's name during a reprimand, just the command NO!! Since dogs don't understand words, comics often use dogs trained with opposite meanings. Thus, when the comic commands his dog to SIT the dog will stand up, and vice versa.

To teach the down/stay, do the down as previously described. As soon as the dog lies down, say 'Stay' and step out on your right foot just as you did in the sit/stay. Count to five and then return to stand beside the dog with him on your left side. Release the treat and praise as always.

Within a week or ten days, you can begin to add a bit of distance between you and your dog when you leave him. When you do, use your left hand open with the palm facing the dog as a stay signal, much the same as the hand signal a constable uses to stop traffic at an intersection.

'WHERE ARE YOU?'

When calling the dog, do not say 'Come.' Say things like, 'Rover, where are you? See if you can find me! I have a biscuit for you!' Keep up a constant line of chatter with coaxing sounds and frequent questions such as, 'Where are you?' The dog will learn to follow the sound of your voice to locate you and receive his reward.

Hold the food treat in your right hand as before, but this time the food is not touching the dog's nose. He will watch the food hand and quickly learn that he is going to get that treat as soon as you return to his side.

When you can stand 1 metre away from your dog for 30 seconds, you can then begin building time and distance in both stays. Eventually, the dog can be expected to remain in the stay position for prolonged periods of time until you return to him or call him to you. Always praise lavishly when he stays.

TEACHING COME

If you make teaching 'come' an exciting experience, you should never have a 'student' that does not love the game or that fails to come when called. The secret, it seems, is never to teach the word 'come.'

At times when an owner most wants his dog to come when called, the owner is likely to be upset or anxious and he allows these feelings to come through in the tone of his voice when he calls his dog. Hearing that desperation in his owner's voice, the dog fears the results of going to him and therefore either disobeys outright or runs in the opposite direction. The secret, therefore, is to teach the dog a game and, when you want him to come to you, simply play the game. It is practically a no-fail solution!

To begin, have several members of your family take a few food treats and each go into a different room in the house. Take turns calling the dog, and each person should celebrate the dog's finding him with a treat and lots of happy praise. When a person calls the dog, he is actually inviting the dog to find him and get a treat as a reward for 'winning.'

'COME' . . . BACK

Never call your dog to come to you for a correction or scold him when he reaches you. That is the quickest way to turn a 'Come' command into 'Go away fast!' Dogs think only in the present tense, and your dog will connect the scolding with coming to you, not with the misbehaviour of a few moments earlier.

A few turns of the 'Where are you?' game and the dog will understand that everyone is playing the game and that each person has a big celebration awaiting his success at locating them. Once he learns to love the game, simply calling out 'Where are you?' will bring him running from wherever he is when he hears that all-important question.

The come command is recognised as one of the most important things to teach a dog, but there are trainers who work with thousands of dogs and never teach the actual word 'Come.' Yet these dogs will race to respond to a person who uses the dog's name followed by 'Where are you?' For example, a woman has a 12-year-old companion dog who went blind, but who never fails to locate her owner when asked, 'Where are you?'

Children, in particular, love to play this game with their dogs. Children can hide in smaller places like a shower or bath, behind a bed or under a table. The dog needs to work a little bit harder to find these hiding places, but when he does he loves to celebrate with a treat and a tussle with a favourite youngster.

TEACHING HEEL

Heeling means that the dog walks beside the owner without pulling. It takes time and

FETCH!
Play fetch games with your puppy in an enclosed area where he can retrieve his toy and bring it back to you. Always use a toy or object designated just for this purpose. Never use a shoe, stocking or other item he may later confuse with those in your wardrobe or underneath your chair.

patience on the owner's part to succeed at teaching the dog that he (the owner) will not proceed unless the dog is walking calmly beside him. Pulling out ahead on the lead is definitely not acceptable.

Begin by holding the lead in your left hand as the dog sits beside your left leg. Move the loop end of the lead to your right hand but keep your left hand short on the lead so it keeps the dog in close next to you.

The Pointer's athleticism makes him a natural for obedience and agility competition. If he can clear a fence like this, he should make short work of the jumps and other obstacles!

Say 'Heel' and step forward on your left foot. Keep the dog close to you and take three steps. Stop and have the dog sit next to you in what we now call the 'heel position.' Praise verbally, but do not touch the dog. Hesitate a moment and begin again with 'Heel,' taking three steps and stopping, at which point the dog is told to sit again.

Your goal here is to have the dog walk those three steps without pulling on the lead. Once he will walk calmly beside you for three steps without pulling, increase the number of

steps you take to five. When he will walk politely beside you while you take five steps, you can increase the length of your walk to ten steps. Keep increasing the length of your stroll until the dog will walk quietly beside you without pulling as long as you want him to heel. When you stop heeling, indicate to the dog that the exercise is over by verbally praising as you pet him and say 'OK, good dog.' The 'OK' is used as a release word meaning that the exercise is finished and the dog is free to relax.

If you are dealing with a dog who insists on pulling you around, simply 'put on your brakes' and stand your ground until the dog realises that the two of you are not going anywhere until he is beside you and moving at your pace, not his. It may take some time just standing there to convince the dog that you are the leader and you will be the one to decide on the direction and speed of your travel.

Each time the dog looks up at you or slows down to give a slack lead between the two of you, quietly praise him and say, 'Good heel. Good dog.' Eventually, the dog will begin to respond and within a few days he will be walking politely beside you without pulling on the lead. At first, the training sessions should be kept short and very positive; soon the dog will be able to walk nicely with you for increasingly longer distances. Remember also to give the dog free time and the opportunity to run and play when you have finished heel practice.

WEANING OFF FOOD IN TRAINING

Food is used in training new behaviours. Once the dog understands what behaviour goes with a specific command, it is time to start weaning him off the food treats. At first, give a treat after each exercise. Then, start to give a treat only after every other exercise. Mix up the times when you offer a food reward and the times when you only offer praise so that the dog will never know when he is going to receive both food and praise and when he is going to receive only praise. This is called a variable ratio reward system and it proves successful because there is always the chance that the owner will produce a treat, so the dog never stops trying for that reward. No matter what, ALWAYS give verbal praise.

OBEDIENCE CLASSES

It is a good idea to enrol in an obedience class if one is available in your area. If yours is

HEELING WELL
Teach your dog to HEEL in an enclosed area. Once you think the dog will obey reliably and you want to attempt advanced obedience exercises such as off-lead heeling, test him in a fenced-in area so he cannot run away.

a show dog, ringcraft classes would be more appropriate. Many areas have dog clubs that offer basic obedience training as well as preparatory classes for obedience competition. There are also local dog trainers who offer similar classes.

At obedience trials, dogs can earn titles at various levels of competition. The beginning levels of competition include basic behaviours such as sit, down, heel, etc. The more advanced levels of competition include jumping, retrieving, scent discrimination and signal work. The advanced levels require a dog and owner to put a lot of time and effort into their training and the titles that can be earned at these levels of competition are very prestigious.

OTHER ACTIVITIES FOR LIFE
Whether a dog is trained in the structured environment of a class or alone with his owner at home, there are many activities that can bring fun and rewards to both owner and dog once they have mastered basic control.

Teaching the dog to help out around the home, in the garden or on the farm provides great satisfaction to both dog and owner. In addition, the dog's help makes life a little easier for his owner and raises his stature as a valued companion to his family. It helps give the dog a purpose by occupying his mind and providing an outlet for his energy.

If you are interested in participating in organised competition with your Pointer, there are activities other than obedience in which you and your dog can become involved. Agility is a popular sport where

> **OBEDIENCE SCHOOL**
> Taking your dog to an obedience school may be the best investment in time and money you can ever make. You will enjoy the benefits for the lifetime of your dog and you will have the opportunity to meet people with your similar expectations for companion dogs.

dogs run through an obstacle course that includes various jumps, tunnels and other exercises to test the dog's speed and coordination. The owners run beside their dogs to give commands and to guide them through the course. Although competitive, the focus is on fun—it's fun to do, fun to watch and great exercise.

Pointer breeders take great pride in perpetuating the hunting instincts and abilities of their dogs. Pointers make excellent hunting companions for the casual weekend sportsman as well as for the field trial aficionado. The world of field trials is a very exciting and demanding existence. For the Pointer owner who may be interested, you should attend a trial to observe and introduce yourself to the participants. Most field trial participants are personable and helpful and should be able to 'point' you in the right direction.

First Aid at a Glance

Burns
Place the affected area under cool water; use ice if only a small area is burnt.

Bee/Insect bites
Apply ice to relieve swelling; antihistamine dosed properly.

Animal bites
Clean any bleeding area; apply pressure until bleeding subsides; go to the vet.

Spider bites
Use cold compress and a pressurised pack to inhibit venom's spreading.

Antifreeze poisoning
Induce vomiting with hydrogen peroxide. Seek *immediate* veterinary help!

Fish hooks
Removal best handled by vet; hook must be cut in order to remove.

Snake bites
Pack ice around bite; contact vet quickly; identify snake for proper antivenin.

Car accident
Move dog from roadway with blanket; seek veterinary aid.

Shock
Calm the dog, keep him warm; seek immediate veterinary help.

Nosebleed
Apply cold compress to the nose; apply pressure to any visible abrasion.

Bleeding
Apply pressure above the area; treat wound by applying a cotton pack.

Heat stroke
Submerge dog in cold bath; cool down with fresh air and water; go to the vet.

Frostbite/Hypothermia
Warm the dog with a warm bath, electric blankets or hot water bottles.

Abrasions
Clean the wound and wash out thoroughly with fresh water; apply antiseptic.

 Remember: an injured dog may attempt to bite a helping hand from fear and confusion. Always muzzle the dog before trying to offer assistance.

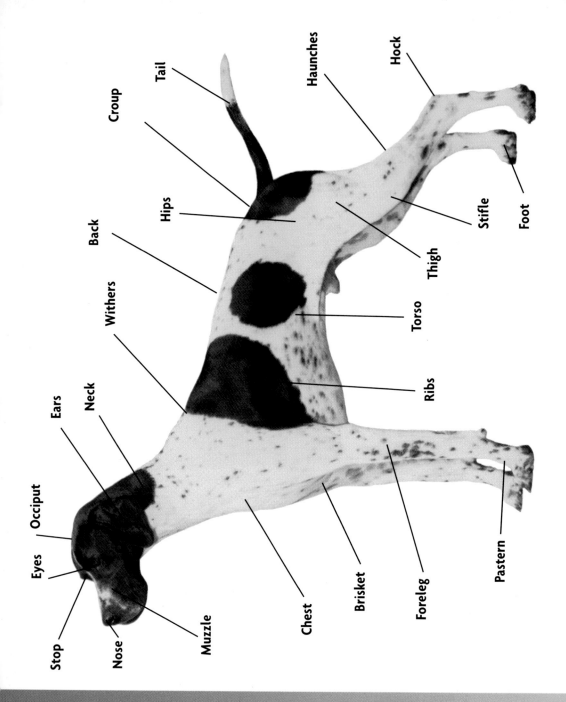

Haunches

Hock

Tail

Croup

Stifle

Thigh

Foot

Hips

Back

Torso

Withers

Ribs

Ears

Neck

Occiput

Eyes

Chest

Brisket

Foreleg

Pastern

Stop

Nose

Muzzle

Physical Structure of the Pointer

Health Care of Your
POINTER

Dogs suffer many of the same physical illnesses as people. They might even share many of the same psychological problems. Since people usually know more about human diseases than canine maladies, many of the terms used in this chapter will be familiar but not necessarily those used by veterinary surgeons. We will use the term *x-ray*, instead of the more acceptable term *radiograph*. We will also use the familiar term *symptoms* even though dogs don't have symptoms, which are verbal descriptions of the patient's feelings; dogs have *clinical signs*. Since dogs can't speak, we have to look for clinical signs...but we still use the term *symptoms* in this book.

As a general rule, medicine is *practised*. That term is not arbitrary. Medicine is a constantly changing art as we learn more and more about genetics, electronic aids (like CAT scans) and daily laboratory advances. There are many dog maladies, like canine hip dysplasia, which are not universally treated in the same manner. Some veterinary surgeons opt for surgery more often than others do.

SELECTING A VETERINARY SURGEON

Your selection of a veterinary surgeon should not be based upon personality (as most are) but upon their convenience to your home. You want a vet who is close because you might have emergencies or need to make multiple visits for treatments. You want a vet who has services that you might require such as tattooing and grooming, as well as sophisticated pet supplies and a good reputation for ability and responsiveness. There is nothing more frustrating than having to wait a day or more to get a response from your veterinary surgeon.

All veterinary surgeons are

Before you buy a Pointer puppy, meet and interview the veterinary surgeons in your area. Take everything into consideration. Discuss his background, specialities, fees, emergency policies, office hours, etc.

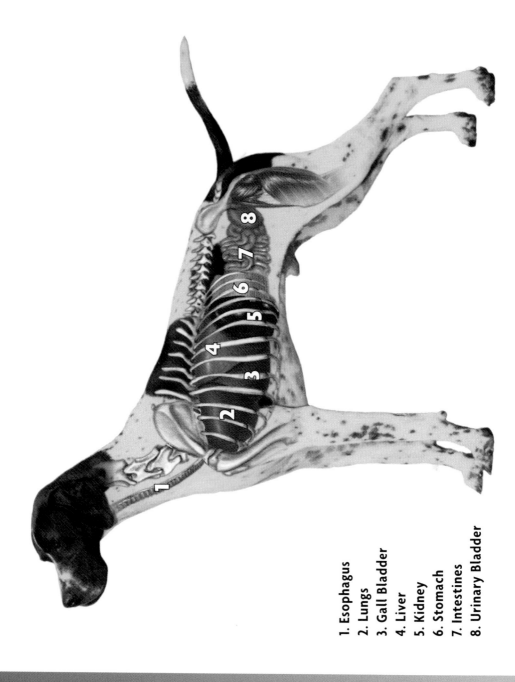

1. Esophagus
2. Lungs
3. Gall Bladder
4. Liver
5. Kidney
6. Stomach
7. Intestines
8. Urinary Bladder

Internal Organs of the Pointer

licensed and their diplomas and/or certificates should be displayed in their waiting rooms. There are, however, many veterinary specialities that usually require further studies and internships. There are specialists in heart problems (veterinary cardiologists), skin problems (veterinary dermatologists), teeth and gum problems (veterinary dentists), eye problems (veterinary ophthalmologists) and x-rays (veterinary radiologists), as well as vets who have specialities in bones, muscles or other organs. Most veterinary surgeons do routine surgery such as neutering, stitching up wounds and docking tails for those breeds in which such is required for show purposes. When the problem affecting your dog is serious, it is not unusual or impudent to get another medical opinion, although in Britain you are obliged to advise the vets concerned about this. You might also want to compare costs among several veterinary surgeons. Sophisticated health care and veterinary services can be very costly. Important decisions are often based upon financial considerations.

PREVENTATIVE MEDICINE
It is much easier, less costly and more effective to practise preventative medicine than to fight bouts of illness and disease. Properly

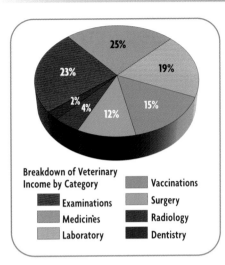

A typical American vet's income, categorised according to services provided. This survey dealt with small-animal practices.

Breakdown of Veterinary Income by Category

- Examinations
- Medicines
- Laboratory
- Vaccinations
- Surgery
- Radiology
- Dentistry

bred puppies come from parents who were selected based upon their genetic disease profile. Their mothers should have been vaccinated, free of all internal and external parasites and properly nourished. For these reasons, a visit to the veterinary surgeon who cared for the dam is recommended. The dam can pass on disease resistance to her puppies, which can last for eight to ten weeks. She can also pass on parasites and many infections. That's why you should visit the veterinary surgeon who cared for the dam.

VACCINATION SCHEDULING
Most vaccinations are given by injection and should only be done by a veterinary surgeon. Both he and you should keep a record of the date of the injection, the identification of the vaccine and

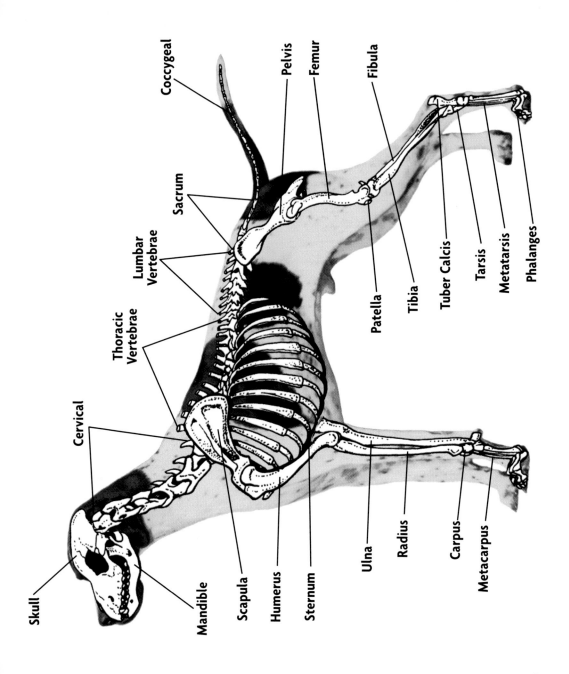

Coccygeal

Pelvis

Femur

Fibula

Sacrum

Lumbar Vertebrae

Patella

Tibia

Tuber Calcis

Tarsis

Metatarsis

Phalanges

Thoracic Vertebrae

Cervical

Skull

Mandible

Scapula

Humerus

Sternum

Ulna

Radius

Carpus

Metacarpus

Skeletal Structure of the Pointer

the amount given. Some vets give a first vaccination at eight weeks, but most dog breeders prefer the course not to commence until about ten weeks because of negating any antibodies passed on by the dam. The vaccination scheduling is usually based on a 15-day cycle. You must take your vet's advice regarding when to vaccinate as this may differ according to the vaccine used. Most vaccinations immunize your puppy against viruses.

The usual vaccines contain immunizing doses of several different viruses such as distemper, parvovirus, parainfluenza and hepatitis although some veterinary surgeons recommend separate vaccines for each disease. There are other vaccines available when the puppy is at risk. You should rely upon professional advice. This is especially true for the booster-shot programme. Most vaccination programmes require a booster

PUPPY VACCINATIONS

Your veterinary surgeon will probably recommend that your puppy be vaccinated before you take him outside. There are airborne diseases, parasite eggs in the grass and unexpected visits from other dogs that might be dangerous to your puppy's health.

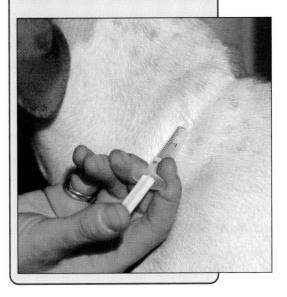

MORE THAN VACCINES

Vaccinations help prevent your new puppy from contracting diseases, but they do not cure them. Proper nutrition as well as parasite control keep your dog healthy and less susceptible to many dangerous diseases. Remember that your dog depends on you to ensure his well-being.

when the puppy is a year old and once a year thereafter. In some cases, circumstances may require more or less frequent immunizations. Kennel cough, more formally known as tracheobronchitis, is treated with a vaccine that is sprayed into the dog's nostrils. Kennel cough is usually included in routine vaccination, but this is often not so effective as for other major diseases.

Normal hairs of a dog enlarged 200 times original size. The cuticle (outer covering) is clean and healthy. Unlike human hair that grows from the base, a dog's hair also grows from the end, as shown in the inset. Scanning electron micrographs by Dr Dennis Kunkel, University of Hawaii.

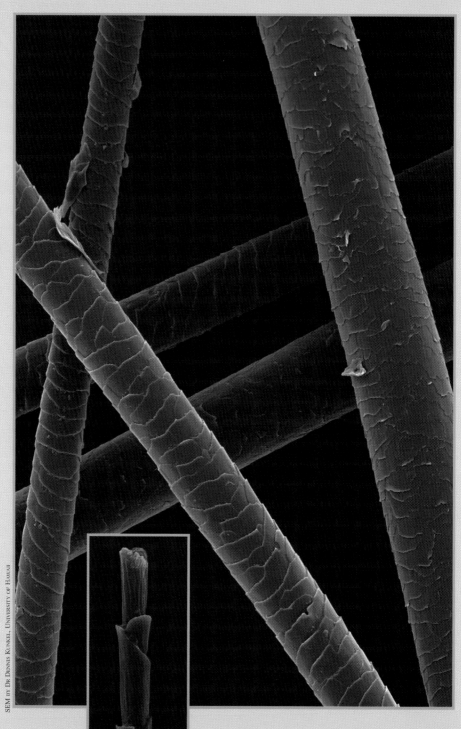

VACCINE ALLERGIES

Vaccines do not work all the time. Sometimes dogs are allergic to them and many times the antibodies, which are supposed to be stimulated by the vaccine, just are not produced. You should keep your dog in the veterinary clinic for an hour after it is vaccinated to be sure there are no allergic reactions.

WEANING TO FIVE MONTHS OLD

Puppies should be weaned by the time they are about two months old. A puppy that remains for at least eight weeks with its mother and littermates usually adapts better to other dogs and people later in its life.

Some new owners have their puppy examined by a veterinary surgeon immediately, which is a good idea. Vaccination programmes usually begin when the puppy is very young.

The puppy will have its teeth examined and have its skeletal conformation and general health checked prior to certification by the veterinary surgeon. Puppies in certain breeds have problems with their kneecaps, cataracts and other eye problems, heart murmurs and undescended testicles. They may also have personality problems and your veterinary surgeon might have training in temperament evaluation.

FIVE TO TWELVE MONTHS OF AGE

Unless you intend to breed or show your dog, neutering the puppy at six months of age is recommended. Discuss this with your veterinary surgeon. Neutering has proven to be extremely beneficial to both male and female puppies. Besides eliminating the possibility of pregnancy, it inhibits (but does not prevent) breast cancer in bitches and prostate cancer in male dogs. Under no circumstances should a bitch be spayed prior to her first season.

Your veterinary surgeon should provide your puppy with a thorough dental evaluation at six months of age, ascertaining whether all the permanent teeth have erupted properly. A home

KNOW WHEN TO POSTPONE A VACCINATION

While the visit to the vet is costly, it is never advisable to update a vaccination when visiting with a sick or pregnant dog. Vaccinations should be avoided for all elderly dogs. If your dog is showing the signs of any illness or any medical condition, no matter how serious or mild, including skin irritations, do not vaccinate. Likewise, a lame dog should never be vaccinated; any dog undergoing surgery, or a dog on any immunosuppressant drugs should not be vaccinated until fully recovered.

HEALTH AND VACCINATION SCHEDULE

AGE IN WEEKS:	6TH	8TH	10TH	12TH	14TH	16TH	20-24TH	1 YR
Worm Control	✔	✔	✔	✔	✔	✔	✔	
Neutering								✔
Heartworm*		✔		✔		✔	✔	
Parvovirus	✔		✔		✔		✔	✔
Distemper		✔		✔		✔		✔
Hepatitis		✔		✔		✔		✔
Leptospirosis								✔
Parainfluenza	✔		✔		✔			✔
Dental Examination		✔					✔	✔
Complete Physical		✔					✔	✔
Coronavirus				✔			✔	✔
Kennel Cough	✔							
Hip Dysplasia								✔
Rabies*							✔	

Vaccinations are not instantly effective. It takes about two weeks for the dog's immunization system to develop antibodies. Most vaccinations require annual booster shots. Your veterinary surgeon should guide you in this regard.
*Not applicable in the United Kingdom

dental care regimen should be initiated at six months, including brushing weekly and providing good dental devices (such as nylon bones). Regular dental care promotes healthy teeth, fresh breath and a longer life.

ONE TO SEVEN YEARS
Once a year, your grown dog should visit the vet for an examination and vaccination boosters, if needed. Some vets recommend blood tests, thyroid level check and dental evaluation to accompany these annual visits. A thorough clinical evaluation by the vet can provide critical background information for your dog. Blood tests are often performed at one year of age, and dental examinations around the third or fourth birthday. In the long run, quality preventative care for your pet can save money, teeth and lives.

SKIN PROBLEMS IN POINTERS
Veterinary surgeons are consulted by dog owners for skin problems more than any other group of diseases or maladies. Dogs' skin is almost as sensitive as human skin and both suffer almost the same ailments. (Though the occurrence of acne in dogs is rare!) For this reason, veterinary dermatology has developed into a

speciality practised by many veterinary surgeons.

Since many skin problems have visual symptoms that are almost identical, it requires the skill of an experienced veterinary dermatologist to identify and cure many of the more severe skin disorders. Pet shops sell many treatments for skin problems but most of the treatments are directed at symptoms and not the underlying problem(s). If your dog is suffering from a skin disorder, you should seek profes-sional assistance as quickly as possible. As with all diseases, the earlier a problem is identified and treated, the more successful is the cure.

HEREDITARY SKIN DISORDERS

Veterinary dermatologists are currently researching a number of skin disorders that are believed to have a hereditary basis. These inherited diseases are transmitted by both parents, who appear (phenotypically) normal but have a recessive gene for the disease,

DISEASE REFERENCE CHART

	What is it?	What causes it?	Symptoms
Leptospirosis	Severe disease that affects the internal organs; can be spread to people.	A bacterium, which is often carried by rodents, that enters through mucous membranes and spreads quickly throughout the body.	Range from fever, vomiting and loss of appetite in less severe cases to shock, irreversible kidney damage and possibly death in most severe cases.
Rabies	Potentially deadly virus that infects warm-blooded mammals. Not seen in United Kingdom.	Bite from a carrier of the virus, mainly wild animals.	1st stage: dog exhibits change in behaviour, fear. 2nd stage: dog's behaviour becomes more aggressive. 3rd stage: loss of coordination, trouble with bodily functions.
Parvovirus	Highly contagious virus, potentially deadly.	Ingestion of the virus, which is usually spread through the faeces of infected dogs.	Most common: severe diarrhoea. Also vomiting, fatigue, lack of appetite.
Kennel cough	Contagious respiratory infection.	Combination of types of bacteria and virus. Most common: *Bordetella bronchiseptica* bacteria and parainfluenza virus.	Chronic cough.
Distemper	Disease primarily affecting respiratory and nervous system.	Virus that is related to the human measles virus.	Mild symptoms such as fever, lack of appetite and mucous secretion progress to evidence of brain damage, 'hard pad.'
Hepatitis	Virus primarily affecting the liver.	Canine adenovirus type I (CAV-1). Enters system when dog breathes in particles.	Lesser symptoms include listlessness, diarrhoea, vomiting. More severe symptoms include 'blue-eye' (clumps of virus in eye).
Coronavirus	Virus resulting in digestive problems.	Virus is spread through infected dog's faeces.	Stomach upset evidenced by lack of appetite, vomiting, diarrhoea.

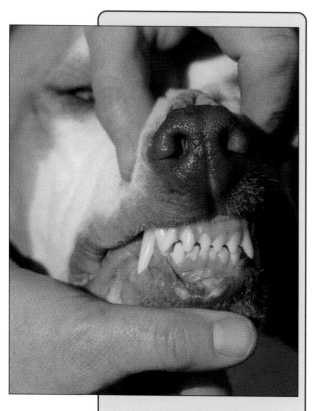

meaning that they carry, but are not affected by, the disease. These diseases pose serious problems to breeders because in some instances there is no method of identifying carriers. Often the secondary diseases associated with these skin conditions are even more debilitating than the disorder itself, including cancers and respiratory problems; others can be lethal.

Among the hereditary skin disorders, for which the mode of inheritance is known, are: acrodermatitis, cutaneous asthenia (Ehlers-Danlos syndrome), sebaceous adenitis, cyclic hematopoiesis, dermatomyositis, IgA deficiency, colour dilution alopecia and nodular dermatofibrosis. Some of these disorders are limited to one or two breeds and others affect a large number

CARETAKER OF TEETH

You are your dog's caretaker and his dentist. Vets warn that plaque and tartar buildup on the teeth will damage the gums and allow bacteria to enter the dog's bloodstream, causing serious damage to the animal's vital organs. Studies show that over 50 percent of dogs have some form of gum disease before age three. Daily or weekly tooth cleaning (with a brush or soft gauze pad wipes) can add years to your dog's life.

'P' STANDS FOR PROBLEM

Urinary tract disease is a serious condition that requires immediate medical attention. Symptoms include urinating in inappropriate places or the need to urinate frequently in small amounts. Urinary tract disease is most effectively treated with antibiotics. To help promote good urinary tract health, owners must always be sure that a constant supply of fresh water is available to their pets.

BE CAREFUL WHERE YOU WALK YOUR DOG

Dogs who have been exposed to lawns sprayed with herbicides have double and triple the rate of malignant lymphoma. Town dogs are especially at risk, as they are exposed to tailored lawns and gardens. Dogs perspire and absorb through their footpads. Be careful where your dog walks and always avoid any area that appears yellowed from chemical overspray.

of breeds. All inherited diseases must be diagnosed and treated by a veterinary specialist.

PARASITE BITES

Many of us are allergic to insect bites. The bites itch, erupt and may even become infected. Dogs have the same reaction to fleas, ticks and/or mites. When an insect lands on you, you have the chance to whisk it away with your hand. Unfortunately, when your dog is bitten by a flea, tick or mite, it can only scratch it away or bite it. By the time the dog has been bitten, the parasite has done some of its damage. It may also have laid eggs to cause further problems in the near future. The itching from parasite bites is probably due to the saliva injected into the site when the parasite sucks the dog's blood.

AUTO-IMMUNE SKIN CONDITIONS

Auto-immune skin conditions are commonly referred to as being allergic to yourself, while allergies are usually inflammatory reactions to an outside stimulus. Auto-immune diseases cause serious damage to the tissues that are involved.

The best known auto-immune disease is lupus, which affects people as well as dogs. The symptoms are variable and may affect the kidneys, bones, blood chemistry and skin. It can be fatal to both dogs and humans, though it is not thought to be transmissible. It is usually successfully treated with cortisone, prednisone or a similar corticosteroid, but extensive use of these drugs can have harmful side effects.

ACRAL LICK GRANULOMA

Many large dogs have a very poorly understood syndrome called acral lick granuloma. The manifestation of the problem is the dog's tireless attack at a specific area of the body, almost always the legs or paws. They lick so intensively that they remove the hair and skin, leaving an ugly,

THE SAME ALLERGIES

Chances are that you and your dog will have the same allergies. Your allergies are readily recognisable and usually easily treated. Your dog's allergies may be masked.

large wound. Tiny protuberances, which are outgrowths of new capillaries, bead on the surface of the wound. Owners who notice their dogs' biting and chewing at their extremities should have the vet determine the cause. If lick granuloma is identified, although there is no absolute cure, corticosteroids are the most common treatment.

Airborne Allergies

An interesting allergy is pollen allergy. Humans have hay fever, rose fever and other fevers with which they suffer during the pollinating season. Many dogs suffer the same allergies. When the pollen count is high, your dog might suffer but don't expect him to sneeze and have a runny nose like humans. Dogs react to pollen allergies the same way they react to fleas—they scratch and bite themselves.

Dogs, like humans, can be tested for allergens. Discuss the testing with your veterinary dermatologist.

FOOD PROBLEMS

FOOD ALLERGIES
Dogs are allergic to many foods that are best-sellers and highly recommended by breeders and veterinary surgeons. Changing the brand of food that you buy may not eliminate the problem if the element to which the dog is allergic is contained in the new brand.

Recognising a food allergy is difficult. Humans vomit or have rashes when they eat a food to which they are allergic. Dogs neither vomit nor (usually) develop a rash. They react in the same manner as they do to an airborne or flea allergy; they itch, scratch and bite, thus making the diagnosis extremely difficult. While pollen allergies and parasite bites are usually seasonal, food allergies are year-round problems.

FOOD INTOLERANCE
Food intolerance is the inability of the dog to completely digest certain foods. Puppies that may have done very well on their mother's milk may not do well on cow's milk. The rest of this food intolerance may be loose bowels, passing gas and stomach pains. These are the only obvious symptoms of food intolerance and that makes diagnosis difficult.

TREATING FOOD PROBLEMS
It is possible to handle food allergies and food intolerance yourself. Put your dog on a diet that it has never had. Obviously if it has never eaten this new food it can't have been allergic or intolerant of it. Start with a single ingredient that is not in the dog's diet at the present time. Ingredients like chopped beef or fish are common in dogs' diets, so try something more exotic like rabbit, pheasant or even just vegetables. Keep the dog on this diet (with no additives) for a month. If the symptoms of food allergy or intolerance disappear, chances are your dog has a food allergy.

Don't think that the single ingredient cured the problem. You still must find a suitable diet and ascertain which ingredient in the old diet was objectionable. This is most easily done by adding ingredients to the new diet one at a time. Let the dog stay on the modified diet for a month before you add another ingredient. Eventually, you will determine the ingredient that caused the adverse reaction.

An alternative method is to carefully study the ingredients in the diet to which your dog is allergic or intolerant. Identify the main ingredient in this diet and eliminate the main ingredient by buying a different food that does not have that ingredient. Keep experimenting until the symptoms disappear after one month on the new diet.

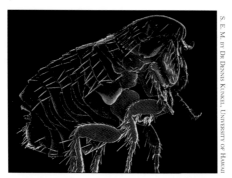

A scanning electron micrograph (S. E. M.) of a dog flea, *Ctenocephalides canis.*

S. E. M. BY DR DENNIS KUNKEL, UNIVERSITY OF HAWAII

Magnified head of a dog flea, *Ctenocephalides canis.*

S. E. M. BY DR DENNIS KUNKEL, UNIVERSITY OF HAWAII

A male dog flea, *Ctenocephalides canis.*

EXTERNAL PARASITES

Of all the problems to which dogs are prone, none is more well known and frustrating than fleas. Flea infestation is relatively simple to cure but difficult to prevent. Parasites that are harboured inside the body are a bit more difficult to eradicate but they are easier to control.

FLEAS

To control a flea infestation you have to understand the flea's life cycle. Fleas are often thought of as a summertime problem but centrally heated homes have changed the patterns and fleas can be found at any time of the year. The most effective method of flea control is a two-stage approach:

PHOTO BY JEAN CLAUDE REVY/PHOTOTAKE.

FLEA-KILLERS

Flea-killers are poisonous. You should not spray these toxic chemicals on areas of a dog's body that he licks, on his genitals or on his face. Flea killers taken internally are a better answer, but check with your vet in case internal therapy is not advised for your dog.

one stage to kill the adult fleas, and the other to control the development of pre-adult fleas. Unfortunately, no single active ingredient is effective against all stages of the life cycle.

LIFE CYCLE STAGES

During its life, a flea will pass through four life stages: egg, larva, pupa and adult. The adult stage is the most visible and irritating stage of the flea life cycle and this is why the majority of flea-control products concentrate on this stage. The fact is that adult fleas account for only 1% of the total flea population, and the other 99% exist in pre-adult stages, i.e. eggs, larvae and pupae. The pre-adult stages are barely visible to the naked eye.

THE LIFE CYCLE OF THE FLEA

Eggs are laid on the dog, usually in quantities of about 20 or 30, several times a day. The female adult flea must have a blood meal before each egg-laying session. When first laid, the eggs will cling to the dog's fur, as the eggs are still moist. However, they will quickly dry out and fall from the dog, especially if the dog moves around or scratches. Many eggs will fall off in the dog's favourite area or an area in which he spends a lot of time, such as his bed.

Once the eggs fall from the dog onto the carpet or furniture, they will hatch into larvae. This takes from one to ten days. Larvae are not particularly mobile, and will usually travel only a few inches from where they hatch. However, they do have a tendency to move

A Look at Fleas

Fleas have been around for millions of years and have adapted to changing host animals.
They are able to go through a complete life cycle in less than one month or they can extend their lives to almost two years by remaining as pupae or cocoons. They do not need blood or any other food for up to 20 months.
They have been measured as being able to jump 300,000 times and can jump 150 times their length in any direction including straight up. Those are just a few of the reasons why they are so successful in infesting a dog!

ILLUSTRATION COURTESY OF BAYER VITAL GMBH & CO. KG

away from light and heavy traffic—under furniture and behind doors are common places to find high quantities of flea larvae.

The flea larvae feed on dead organic matter, including adult flea faeces, until they are ready to change into adult fleas. Fleas will usually remain as larvae for around seven days. After this period, the larvae will pupate into protective pupae. While inside the pupae, the larvae will undergo metamorphosis and change into adult fleas. This can take as little time as a few days, but the adult fleas can remain inside the pupae waiting to hatch for up to two years. The pupae are signalled to hatch by certain stimuli, such as physical pressure—the pupae's being stepped on, heat from an animal lying on the pupae or increased carbon dioxide levels and vibrations—indicating that a suitable host is available.

Once hatched, the adult flea must feed within a few days. Once the adult flea finds a host, it will not leave voluntarily. It only becomes dislodged by grooming or

EN GARDE: CATCHING FLEAS OFF GUARD

Consider the following ways to arm yourself against fleas:
- Add a small amount of pennyroyal or eucalyptus oil to your dog's bath. These natural remedies repel fleas.
- Supplement your dog's food with fresh garlic (minced or grated) and a hearty amount of brewer's yeast, both of which ward off fleas.
- Use a flea comb on your dog daily. Submerge fleas in a cup of bleach to kill them quickly.
- Confine the dog to only a few rooms to limit the spread of fleas in the home.
- Vacuum daily . . . and get all of the crevices! Dispose of the bag every few days until the problem is under control.
- Wash your dog's bedding daily. Cover cushions where your dog sleeps with towels, and wash the towels often.

MIXING CAN BE TOXIC

Never mix flea control products without first consulting your veterinary surgeon. Some products can become toxic when combined with others and can cause serious or fatal consequences.

---

the host animal's scratching. The adult flea will remain on the host for the duration of its life unless forcibly removed.

TREATING THE ENVIRONMENT AND THE DOG

Treating fleas should be a two-pronged attack. First, the environment needs to be treated; this includes carpets and furniture, especially the dog's bedding and

Opposite page: A scanning electron micrograph of a dog or cat flea, *Ctenocephalides*, magnified more than 100x. This image has been colourized for effect.

The Life Cycle of the Flea

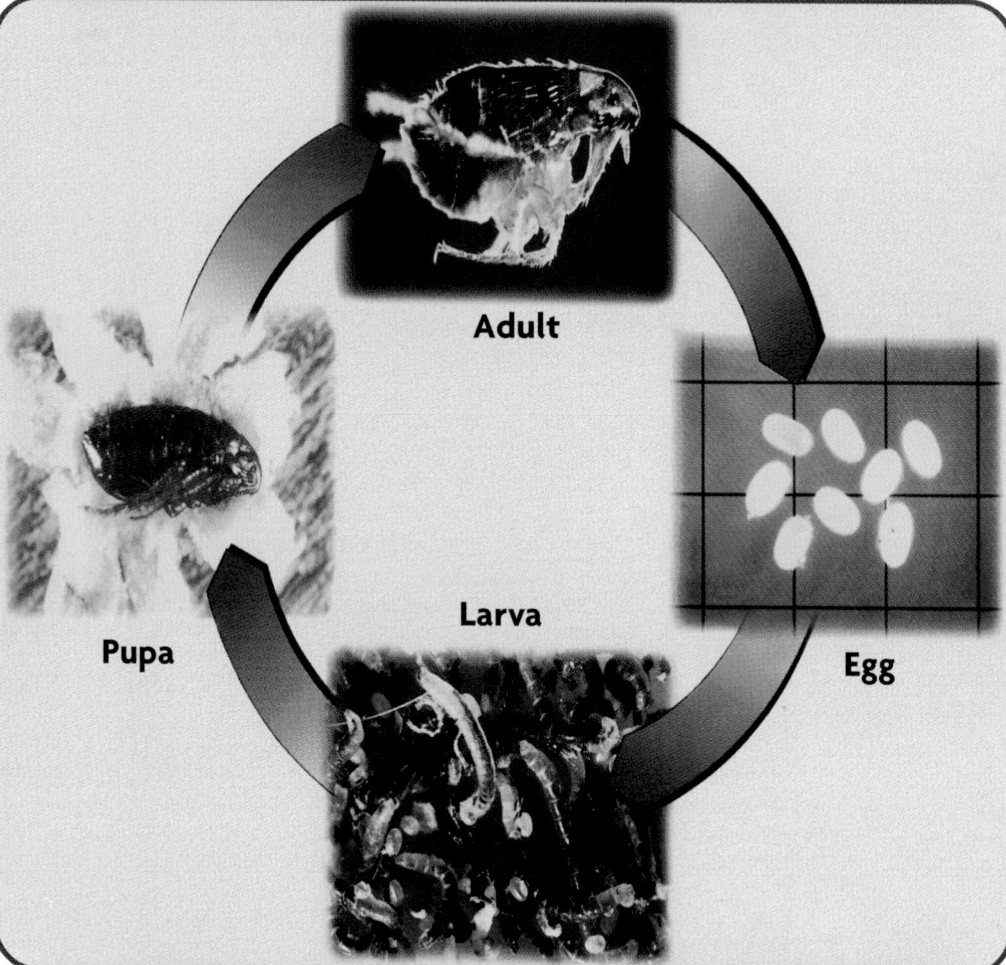

Adult

Pupa

Larva

Egg

areas underneath furniture. The environment should be treated with a household spray containing an Insect Growth Regulator (IGR) and an insecticide to kill the adult fleas. Most IGRs are effective against eggs and larvae; they actually mimic the fleas' own hormones and stop the eggs and larvae from developing into adult fleas. There are currently no treatments available to attack the pupa stage of the life cycle, so the adult insecticide is used to kill the newly hatched adult fleas before

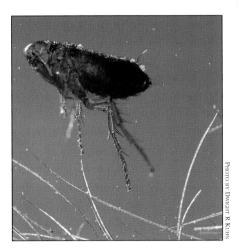

Photo by Dwight R Kuhn

TICKS AND MITES

Though not as common as fleas, ticks and mites are found all over the tropical and temperate world. They don't bite, like fleas; they harpoon. They dig their sharp proboscis (nose) into the dog's skin and drink the blood. Their only food and drink is dog's blood. Dogs can get Lyme disease, Rocky Mountain spotted fever (normally

Dwight R Kuhn's magnificent action photo showing a flea jumping from a dog's back.

they find a host. Most IGRs are active for many months, whilst adult insecticides are only active for a few days.

When treating with a household spray, it is a good idea to vacuum before applying the product. This stimulates as many pupae as possible to hatch into adult fleas. The vacuum cleaner should also be treated with a flea treatment to prevent the eggs and larvae that have been hoovered into the vacuum bag from hatching. The second stage of treatment is to apply an adult insecticide to the dog. Traditionally, this would be in the form of a collar or a spray, but more recent innovations include digestible insecticides that poison the fleas when they ingest the dog's blood. Alternatively, there are drops that, when placed on the back of the animal's neck, spread throughout the fur and skin to kill adult fleas.

FLEA CONTROL

Two types of products should be used when treating fleas—a product to treat the pet and a product to treat the home. Adult fleas represent less than 1% of the flea population. The pre-adult fleas (eggs, larvae and pupae) represent more than 99% of the flea population and are found in the environment; it is in the case of pre-adult fleas that products containing an Insect Growth Regulator (IGR) should be used in the home.

IGRs are a new class of compounds used to prevent the development of insects. They do not kill the insect outright, but instead use the insect's biology against it to stop it from completing its growth. Products that contain methoprene are the world's first and leading IGRs. Used to control fleas and other insects, this type of IGR will stop flea larvae from developing and protect the house for up to seven months.

133

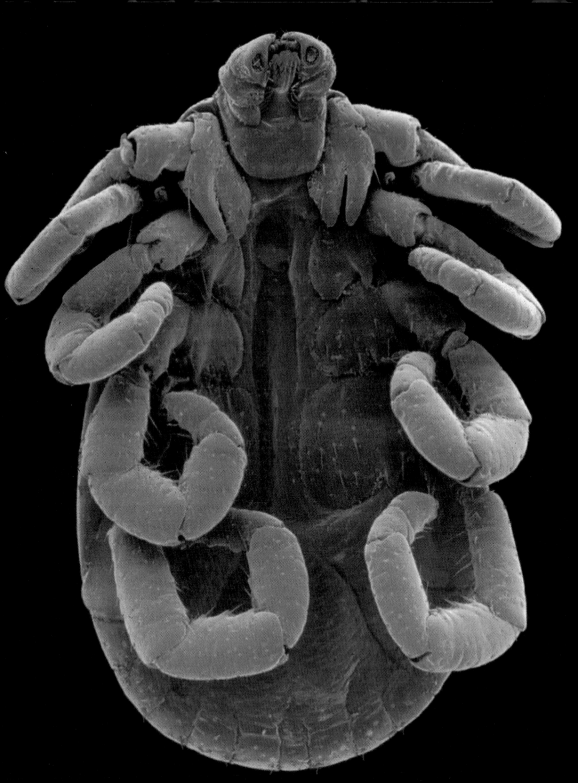

S. E. M. BY DR DENNIS KUNKEL, UNIVERSITY OF HAWAII

found in the US only), paralysis and many other diseases from ticks and mites. They may live where fleas are found and they like to hide in cracks or seams in walls wherever dogs live. They are controlled the same way fleas are controlled. The dog tick, *Dermacentor variabilis*, may well be the most common dog tick in many geographical areas, especially those areas where the climate is hot and humid.

Most dog ticks have life expectancies of a week to six

ILLUSTRATION COURTESY OF BAYER VITAL GMBH & CO. KG

Beware the Deer Tick

The great outdoors may be fun for your dog, but it also is a home to dangerous ticks. Deer ticks carry a bacterium known as *Borrelia burgdorferi* and are most active in the autumn and spring. When infections are caught early, penicillin and tetracycline are effective antibiotics, but if left untreated the bacteria may cause neurological, kidney and cardiac problems as well as long-term trouble with walking and painful joints.

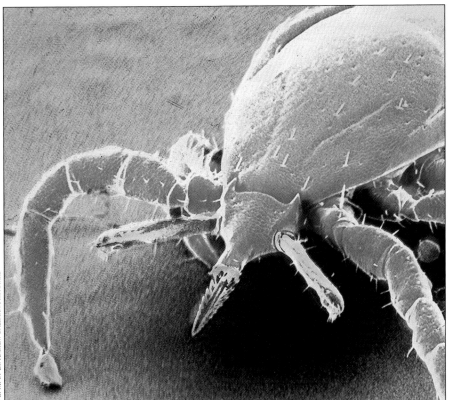

S. E. M. BY DR ANDREW SPIELMAN/PHOTOTAKE

A deer tick, the carrier of Lyme disease. This magnified micrograph has been colourized for effect.

Opposite page: The dog tick, *Dermacentor variabilis*, is probably the most common tick found on dogs. Look at the strength in its eight legs! No wonder it's hard to detach them.

135

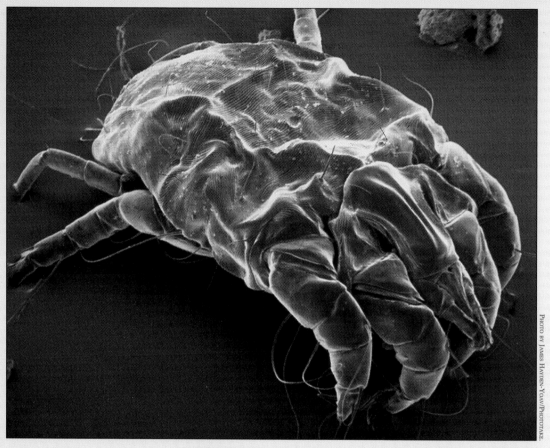

Photo by James Hayden-Yoav/Phototake.

Above:
The mange mite,
Psoroptes bovis.

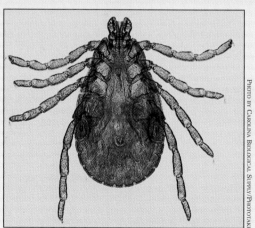

Photo by Carolina Biological Supply/Phototake

A brown dog tick, *Rhipicephalus sanguineus*, is an uncommon but annoying tick found on dogs.

Photo by Dwight R Kuhn

Human lice look like dog lice; the two are closely related.

months, depending upon climatic conditions. They can neither jump nor fly, but they can crawl slowly and can range up to 5 metres (16 feet) to reach a sleeping or unsuspecting dog.

MANGE

Mites cause a skin irritation called mange. Some are contagious, like *Cheyletiella*, ear mites, scabies and chiggers. Mites that cause ear-mite infestations are usually controlled with Lindane, which can only be administered by a vet, followed by Tresaderm at home.

It is essential that your dog be treated for mange as quickly as possible because some forms of mange are transmissible to people.

INTERNAL PARASITES

Most animals—fishes, birds and mammals, including dogs and humans—have worms and other parasites that live inside their bodies. According to Dr Herbert R Axelrod, the fish pathologist, there are two kinds of parasites: dumb and smart. The smart parasites live in peaceful cooperation with their hosts (symbiosis), while the dumb parasites kill their host. Most of the worm infections are relatively easy to control. If they are not controlled they weaken the host dog to the point that other medical problems occur, but they are not dumb parasites.

ROUNDWORMS

The roundworms that infect dogs are scientifically known as *Toxocara canis*. They live in the dog's intestine. The worms shed eggs continually. It has been estimated that a dog produces about 150 grammes of faeces every day. Each gramme of faeces averages 10,000–12,000 eggs of roundworms. There are no known areas in which dogs roam that do not contain roundworm eggs. The greatest danger of roundworms is that they infect people too! It is

DEWORMING

Ridding your puppy of worms is VERY IMPORTANT because certain worms that puppies carry, such as tapeworms and roundworms, can infect humans.

Breeders initiate a deworming programme at or about four weeks of age. The routine is repeated every two or three weeks until the puppy is three months old. The breeder from whom you obtained your puppy should provide you with the complete details of the deworming programme.

Your veterinary surgeon can prescribe and monitor the programme of deworming for you. The usual programme is treating the puppy every 15–20 days until the puppy is positively worm free.

It is advised that you only treat your puppy with drugs that are recommended professionally.

wise to have your dog tested regularly for roundworms.

Pigs also have roundworm infections that can be passed to humans and dogs. The typical roundworm parasite is called *Ascaris lumbricoides*.

HOOKWORMS

The worm *Ancylostoma caninum* is commonly called the dog hookworm. It is dangerous to humans and cats. It also has teeth by which it attaches itself to the intestines of the dog. It changes the site of its attachment about six times a day and the dog loses blood from each detachment, possibly causing iron-deficiency anaemia. Hookworms are easily purged from the dog with many medications. Milbemycin oxime,

ROUNDWORM

Average size dogs can pass 1,360,000 roundworm eggs every day.

For example, if there were only 1 million dogs in the world, the world would be saturated with 1,300 metric tonnes of dog faeces.

These faeces would contain 15,000,000,000 roundworm eggs.

It's known that 7–31% of home gardens and children's play boxes in the US contain roundworm eggs.

Flushing dog's faeces down the toilet is not a safe practice because the usual sewage treatments do not destroy roundworm eggs.

Infected puppies start shedding roundworm eggs at 3 weeks of age. They can be infected by their mother's milk.

The roundworm, *Rhabditis*. The roundworm can infect both dogs and humans.

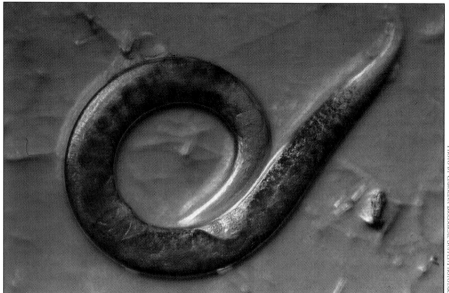

PHOTO BY CAROLINA BIOLOGICAL SUPPLY/PHOTOTAKE

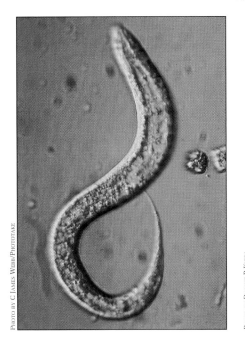

Photo by C James Webb/Phototake

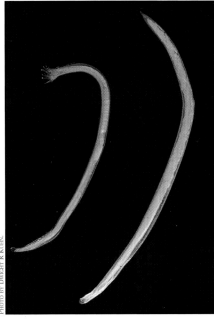

Photo by Dwight R Kuhn.

Left:
The infective
stage of the
hookworm larva.

Right:
Male and female
hookworms,
*Ancylostoma
caninum*, are
uncommonly
found in pet or
show dogs in
Britain.
Hookworms may
infect other dogs
that have exposure
to grasslands.

which also serves as a heartworm preventative in Collies, can be used for this purpose.

In Britain the 'temperate climate' hookworm (*Uncinaria stenocephala*) is rarely found in pet or show dogs, but can occur in hunting packs, racing Greyhounds and sheepdogs because the worms can be prevalent wherever dogs are exercised regularly on grassland.

TAPEWORMS
There are many species of tapeworms. They are carried by fleas! The dog eats the flea and starts the tapeworm cycle. Humans can also be infected with tapeworms, so don't eat fleas! Fleas are so small that your dog could pass them onto your hands, your plate or your food and thus make it possible for you to ingest a flea which is carrying tapeworm eggs.

While tapeworm infection is not life threatening in dogs (smart parasite!), it can be the cause of a

CAUTION: NO SWIMMING!
Never allow your dog to swim in polluted water or public areas where water quality can be suspect. Even perfectly clear water can harbour parasites, many of which can cause serious to fatal illnesses in canines. Areas inhabited by waterfowl and other wildlife are especially dangerous.

139

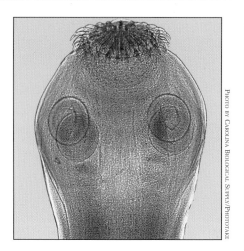

The head and rostellum (the round prominence on the scolex) of a tapeworm, which infects dogs and humans.

PHOTO BY CAROLINA BIOLOGICAL SUPPLY/PHOTOTAKE

very serious liver disease for humans. About 50 percent of the humans infected with *Echinococcus multilocularis*, a type of tapeworm that causes alveolar hydatis, perish.

HEARTWORMS

Heartworms are thin, extended worms up to 30 cms (12 ins) long which live in a dog's heart and the major blood vessels surrounding it. Dogs may have up to 200 worms. Symptoms may be loss of energy, loss of appetite, coughing, the development of a pot belly and anaemia.

Heartworms are transmitted by mosquitoes. The mosquito drinks the blood of an infected dog and takes in larvae with the blood. The larvae, called microfilaria, develop within the body of the mosquito and are passed on to the next dog bitten after the larvae mature. It takes two to three weeks for the larvae to develop to the infective stage within the body of the mosquito. Dogs should be treated at about six weeks of age, and maintained on a prophylactic dose given monthly.

Blood testing for heartworms is not necessarily indicative of how seriously your dog is infected. This is a dangerous disease. Although heartworm is a problem for dogs in America, Australia, Asia and Central Europe, dogs in the United Kingdom are not currently affected by heartworm.

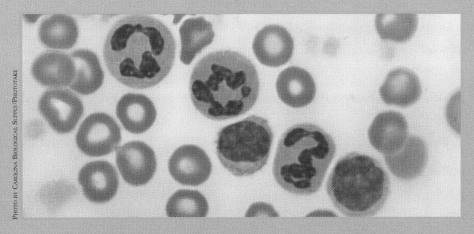

Magnified heartworm larvae, *Dirofilaria immitis.*

PHOTO BY CAROLINA BIOLOGICAL SUPPLY/PHOTOTAKE

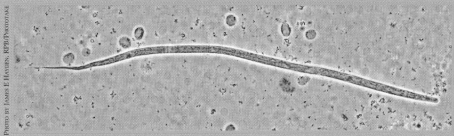

The heartworm, *Dirofilaria immitis.*

PHOTO BY JAMES E HAYDEN, RPB/PHOTOTAKE

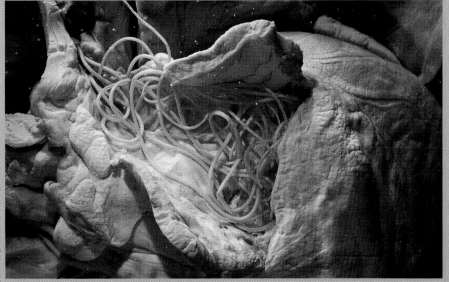

The heart of a dog infected with canine heartworm, *Dirofilaria immitis.*

PHOTO BY JAMES E HAYDEN, RPB/PHOTOTAKE

HOMEOPATHY:
an alternative to conventional medicine

'Less is Most'

Using this principle, the strength of a homeopathic remedy is measured by the number of serial dilutions that were undertaken to create it. The greater the number of serial dilutions, the greater the strength of the homeopathic remedy. The potency of a remedy that has been made by making a dilution of 1 part in 100 parts (or 1/100) is 1c or 1cH. If this remedy is subjected to a series of further dilutions, each one being 1/100, a more dilute and stronger remedy is produced. If the remedy is diluted in this way six times, it is called 6c or 6cH. A dilution of 6c is 1 part in 1000,000,000,000. In general, higher potencies in more frequent doses are better for acute symptoms and lower potencies in more infrequent doses are more useful for chronic, long-standing problems.

CURING OUR DOGS NATURALLY

Holistic medicine means treating the whole animal as a unique, perfect living being. Generally, holistic treatments do not suppress the symptoms that the body naturally produces, as do most medications prescribed by conventional doctors and vets. Holistic methods seek to cure disease by regaining balance and harmony in the patient's environment. Some of these methods include use of nutritional therapy, herbs, flower essences, aromatherapy, acupuncture, massage, chiropractic, and, of course the most popular holistic approach, homeopathy. Homeopathy is a theory or system of treating illness with small doses of substances which, if administered in larger quantities, would produce the symptoms that the patient already has. This approach is often described as 'like cures like.' Although modern veterinary medicine is geared toward the 'quick fix,' homeopathy relies on the belief that, given the time, the body is able to heal itself and return to its natural, healthy state.

Choosing a remedy to cure a problem in our dogs is the difficult part of homeopathy. Consult with your veterinary surgeon for a professional diagnosis of your dog's symptoms. Often these symptoms require immediate conventional

care. If your vet is willing, and somewhat knowledgeable, you may attempt a homeopathic remedy. Be aware that cortisone prevents homeopathic remedies from working. There are hundreds of possibilities and combinations to cure many problems in dogs, from basic physical problems such as excessive moulting, fleas or other parasites, unattractive doggy odour, bad breath, upset tummy, dry, oily or dull coat, diarrhoea, ear problems or eye discharge (including tears and dry or mucousy matter), to behavioural abnormalities, such as fear of loud noises, habitual licking, poor appetite, excessive barking, obesity and various phobias. From alumina to zincum metallicum, the remedies span the planet and the imagination…from flowers and weeds to chemicals, insect droppings, diesel smoke and volcanic ash.

Using 'Like to Treat Like'

Unlike conventional medicines that suppress symptoms, homeopathic remedies treat illnesses with small doses of substances that, if administered in larger quantities, would produce the symptoms that the patient already has. Whilst the same homeopathic remedy can be used to treat different symptoms in different dogs, here are some interesting remedies and their uses.

Apis Mellifica
(made from honey bee venom) can be used for allergies or to reduce swelling that occurs in acutely infected kidneys.

Diesel Smoke
can be used to help control travel sickness.

Calcarea Fluorica
(made from calcium fluoride which helps harden bone structure) can be useful in treating hard lumps in tissues.

Natrum Muriaticum
(made from common salt, sodium chloride) is useful in treating thin, thirsty dogs.

Nitricum Acidum
(made from nitric acid) is used for symptoms you would expect to see from contact with acids such as lesions, especially where the skin joins the linings of body orifices or openings such as the lips and nostrils.

Symphytum
(made from the herb Knitbone, Symphytum officianale) is used to encourage bones to heal.

Urtica Urens
(made from the common stinging nettle) is used in treating painful, irritating rashes.

HOMEOPATHIC REMEDIES FOR YOUR DOG

Symptom/Ailment	Possible Remedy
ALLERGIES	Apis Mellifica 30c, Astacus Fluviatilis 6c, Pulsatilla 30c, Urtica Urens 6c
ALOPECIA	Alumina 30c, Lycopodium 30c, Sepia 30c, Thallium 6c
ANAL GLANDS (BLOCKED)	Hepar Sulphuris Calcareum 30c, Sanicula 6c, Silicea 6c
ARTHRITIS	Rhus Toxicodendron 6c, Bryonia Alba 6c
CATARACT	Calcarea Carbonica 6c, Conium Maculatum 6c, Phosphorus 30c, Silicea 30c
CONSTIPATION	Alumina 6c, Carbo Vegetabilis 30c, Graphites 6c, Nitricum Acidum 30c, Silicea 6c
COUGHING	Aconitum Napellus 6c, Belladonna 30c, Hyoscyamus Niger 30c, Phosphorus 30c
DIARRHOEA	Arsenicum Album 30c, Aconitum Napellus 6c, Chamomilla 30c, Mercurius Corrosivus 30c
DRY EYE	Zincum Metallicum 30c
EAR PROBLEMS	Aconitum Napellus 30c, Belladonna 30c, Hepar Sulphuris 30c, Tellurium 30c, Psorinum 200c
EYE PROBLEMS	Borax 6c, Aconitum Napellus 30c, Graphites 6c, Staphysagria 6c, Thuja Occidentalis 30c
GLAUCOMA	Aconitum Napellus 30c, Apis Mellifica 6c, Phosphorus 30c
HEAT STROKE	Belladonna 30c, Gelsemium Sempervirens 30c, Sulphur 30c
HICCOUGHS	Cinchona Deficinalis 6c
HIP DYSPLASIA	Colocynthis 6c, Rhus Toxicodendron 6c, Bryonia Alba 6c
INCONTINENCE	Argentum Nitricum 6c, Causticum 30c, Conium Maculatum 30c, Pulsatilla 30c, Sepia 30c
INSECT BITES	Apis Mellifica 30c, Cantharis 30c, Hypericum Perforatum 6c, Urtica Urens 30c
ITCHING	Alumina 30c, Arsenicum Album 30c, Carbo Vegetabilis 30c, Hypericum Perforatum 6c, Mezerium 6c, Sulphur 30c
KENNEL COUGH	Drosera 6c, Ipecacuanha 30c
MASTITIS	Apis Mellifica 30c, Belladonna 30c, Urtica Urens 1m
PATELLAR LUXATION	Gelsemium Sempervirens 6c, Rhus Toxicodendron 6c
PENIS PROBLEMS	Aconitum Napellus 30c, Hepar Sulphuris Calcareum 30c, Pulsatilla 30c, Thuja Occidentalis 6c
PUPPY TEETHING	Calcarea Carbonica 6c, Chamomilla 6c, Phytolacca 6c
TRAVEL SICKNESS	Cocculus 6c, Petroleum 6c

Recognising a Sick Dog

Unlike colicky babies and cranky children, our canine kids cannot tell us when they are feeling ill. Therefore, there are a number of signs that owners can identify to know that their dogs are not feeling well.

Take note for physical manifestations such as:

- unusual, bad odour, including bad breath
- excessive moulting
- wax in the ears, chronic ear irritation
- oily, flaky, dull haircoat
- mucous, tearing or similar discharge in the eyes
- fleas or mites
- mucous in stool, diarrhoea
- sensitivity to petting or handling
- licking at paws, scratching face, etc.

Keep an eye out for behavioural changes as well including:

- lethargy, idleness
- lack of patience or general irritability
- lack of appetite, digestive problems
- phobias (fear of people, loud noises, etc.)
- strange behaviour, suspicion, fear
- coprophagia
- more frequent barking
- whimpering, crying

Get Well Soon

You don't need a DVR or a BVMA to provide good TLC to your sick or recovering dog, but you do need to pay attention to some details that normally wouldn't bother him. The following tips will aid Fido's recovery and get him back on his paws again:

- Keep his space free of irritating smells, like heavy perfumes and air fresheners.
- Rest is the best medicine! Avoid harsh lighting that will prevent your dog from sleeping. Shade him from bright sunlight during the day and dim the lights in the evening.
- Keep the noise level down. Animals are more sensitive to sound when they are sick.

- Be attentive to any necessary temperature adjustments. A dog with a fever needs a cool room and cold liquids. A bitch that is whelping or recovering from surgery will be more comfortable in a warm room, consuming warm liquids and food.
- You wouldn't send a sick child back to school early, so don't rush your dog back into a full routine until he seems absolutely ready.

Showing Your POINTER

When you purchased your Pointer you should have made it clear to the breeder whether you wanted one just as a loveable companion and pet, or if you hoped to be buying a Pointer with show prospects. No reputable breeder will sell you a young puppy saying that it is definitely of show quality, for so much can go wrong during the early months of a puppy's development. If you plan to show, what you will hopefully have acquired is a puppy with 'show potential.'

FCI INFORMATION

There are 330 breeds recognised by the FCI, and each breed is considered to be 'owned' by a specific country. Each breed standard is a cooperative effort between the breed's country and the FCI's Standards and Scientific Commissions. Judges use these official breed standards at shows held in FCI member countries. One of the functions of the FCI is to update and translate the breed standards into French, English, Spanish and German.

To the novice, exhibiting a Pointer in the show ring may look easy but it takes a lot of hard work and devotion to do top winning at a show such as the prestigious Crufts, not to mention a little luck too!

The first concept that the canine novice learns when watching a dog show is that each dog first competes against members of its own breed. Once the judge has selected the best member of each breed, provided that the show is judged on a Group system, that chosen dog will compete with other dogs in its group. Finally the best of each group will compete for Best in Show and Reserve Best in Show.

The second concept that you must understand is that the dogs are not actually competing against one another. The judge compares each dog against the breed standard, which is a written description of the ideal specimen of the breed. While some early breed standards were indeed based on specific dogs that were famous or popular, many dedicated enthusiasts say that a

INFORMATION ON CLUBS

You can get information about dog shows from kennel clubs and breed clubs:

Fédération Cynologique Internationale
14, rue Leopold II, B-6530 Thuin, Belgium
www.fci.be

The Kennel Club
1-5 Clarges St., Piccadilly, London W1Y 8AB, UK
www.the-kennel-club.org.uk

American Kennel Club
5580 Centerview Drive,
Raleigh, NC 27606-3390, USA
www.akc.org

Canadian Kennel Club
89 Skyway Ave., Suite 100,
Etobicoke, Ontario M9W 6R4 Canada
www.ckc.ca

and special events, all of which could be of interest, even if you are only an onlooker. Clubs also send out newsletters and some organise training days and seminars in order that people may learn more about their chosen breed. To locate the breed club closest to you, contact The Kennel Club, the ruling body for the British dog world. The Kennel Club governs not only conformation shows but also working trials, obedience trials, agility trials and field trials. The Kennel Club furnishes the rules and regulations for all these events plus

Ch Kinnike CP Schofield, JH, CD is an American champion shown here finishing his obedience title at 10 years of age!

perfect specimen, described in the standard, has never walked into a show ring, has never been bred and, to the woe of dog breeders around the globe, does not exist. Breeders attempt to get as close to this ideal as possible, with every litter, but theoretically the 'perfect' dog is so elusive that it is impossible. (And if the 'perfect' dog were born, breeders and judges would never agree that it was indeed 'perfect.')

If you are interested in exploring dog shows, your best bet is to join your local breed club. These clubs often host both Championship and Open Shows, and sometimes Match meetings

> **DID YOU KNOW?**
> The FCI *does not* issue pedigrees. The FCI members and contract partners are responsible for issuing pedigrees and training judges in their own countries. The FCI does maintain a list of judges and makes sure that they are recognised throughout the FCI member countries.
>
> The FCI also *does not* act as a breeder referral; breeder information is available from FCI-recognised national canine societies in each of the FCI's member countries.

general dog registration and other basic requirements of dog ownership. Its annual show, called the Crufts Dog Show, held in Birmingham, is the largest benched show in England. Every year over 20,000 of the UK's best dogs qualify to participate in this marvellous show which lasts four days.

The Kennel Club governs many different kinds of shows in Great Britain, Australia, South Africa and beyond. At the most competitive and prestigious of these shows, the Championship Shows, a dog can earn Challenge Certificates, and thereby become a Show Champion or a Champion. A dog must earn three Challenge Certificates under three different judges to earn the prefix of 'Sh Ch' or 'Ch' Note that some breeds must also qualify in a field trial in

order to gain the title of full champion. Challenge Certificates are awarded to a very small percentage of the dogs competing, and dogs that are already Champions compete with others for these coveted CCs. The number of Challenge Certificates awarded in any one year is based upon the total number of dogs in each breed entered for competition. There are three types of Championship Shows: an all-breed General Championship Show for all Kennel-Club-recognised breeds; a Group Championship Show that is limited to breeds within one of the groups; and a Breed Show that is usually confined to a single breed. The Kennel Club determines which breeds at which Championship Shows will have the opportunity to earn Challenge Certificates (or tickets). Serious exhibitors often will opt not to participate if the tickets are withheld at a particular show. This policy makes earning championships even more difficult to accomplish.

Open Shows are generally less competitive and are frequently used as 'practice shows' for young dogs. There are hundreds of Open Shows each year that can be delightful social events and are great first show experiences for the novice. Even if you're considering just watching a show to wet your paws, an Open Show is a great choice.

While Championship and Open Shows are most important for the beginner to understand, there are other types of shows in which the interested dog owner can participate. Training clubs sponsor Matches that can be entered on the day of the show for a nominal fee. In these introductory-level exhibitions, two dogs are pulled out of a hat and 'matched,' the winner of that match goes on to the next round, and eventually only one dog is left undefeated.

Exemption Shows are much more light-hearted affairs with usually only four pedigree classes and several 'fun' classes, all of which can be entered on the day. Exemption Shows are sometimes held in conjunction with small agricultural shows and the proceeds must be given to a charity. Limited Shows are also available in small number, but entry is restricted to members of the club which hosts the show, although one can usually join the club when making an entry.

Before you actually step into the ring, you would be well advised to sit back and observe the judge's ring procedure. If it is your first time in the ring, do not be over-anxious and run to the front of the line. It is much better to stand back and study how the exhibitor in front of you is performing. The judge asks each

CLASSES AT DOG SHOWS

There can be as many as 18 classes per sex for your breed. Check the show schedule carefully to make sure that you have entered your dog in the appropriate class. Among the classes offered can be: Beginners; Minor Puppy (ages 6 to 9 months); Puppy (ages 6 to 12 months); Junior (ages 6 to 18 months); Beginners (handler or dog never won first place) as well as the following, each of which is defined in the schedule: Maiden; Novice; Tyro; Debutant; Undergraduate; Graduate; Postgraduate; Minor Limit; Mid Limit; Limit; Open; Veteran; Stud Dog; Brood Bitch; Progeny; Brace and Team.

handler to 'stand' the dog, hopefully showing the dog off to his best advantage. The judge will observe the dog from a distance and from different angles, approach the dog, check his teeth, overall structure, alertness and muscle tone, as well as consider how well the dog 'conforms' to the standard. Most importantly, the judge will have the exhibitor move the dog around the ring in some pattern that he or she should specify (another advantage to not going first, but always listen since some judges change their directions, and the judge is always right!). Finally the judge will give the dog one last look before moving on to the next exhibitor.

If you are not in the top three at your first show, do not be discouraged. Be patient and consistent and you may eventually find yourself in the winning line-up. Remember that the winners were once in your shoes and have devoted many hours and much money to earn the placement. If you find that your dog is losing every time and never getting a nod, it may be time to consider a different dog sport or just enjoy your Pointer as a pet.

WORKING TRIALS
Working trials can be entered by any well-trained dog of any breed, not just Gundogs or Working dogs. Many dogs that earn the Kennel Club Good Citizen Dog award choose to participate in a working trial.

There are five stakes at both open and championship levels: Companion Dog (CD), Utility Dog (UD), Working Dog (WD), Tracking Dog (TD) and Patrol Dog (PD). As in conformation shows, dogs compete against a standard and if the dog reaches the qualifying mark, it obtains a certificate. Divided into groups, each exercise must be achieved 70 percent in order for the dog to qualify. If the dog achieves 80 percent in the open level, it receives a Certificate of Merit (COM); in the championship level, it receives a Qualifying Certificate. At the CD stake, dogs must participate in four groups: Control, Stay, Agility and Search (Retrieve and Nosework). At the next three levels, UD, WD and TD, there are only three groups: Control, Agility and Nosework.

Agility consists of three jumps: a vertical scale up a six-foot wall of planks; a clear jump over a basic three-foot hurdle with a removable top bar; and a long jump across angled planks stretching nine feet.

To earn the UD, WD and TD, dogs must track approximately one-half mile for articles laid from one-half hour to three hours previously. Tracks consist of turns and legs, and fresh ground is used for each participant.

The fifth stake, PD, involves teaching manwork, which is not recommended for every breed.

FIELD TRIALS AND WORKING TESTS

Working tests are frequently used to prepare dogs for field trials, the purpose of which is to heighten the instincts and natural abilities of gundogs. Live game is not used in working tests. Unlike field trials, working tests do not count toward a dog's record at The Kennel Club, though the same judges often oversee working tests. Field trials began in England in 1947 and are only moderately popular amongst dog folk. While breeders of Working and Gundog breeds concern themselves with the field abilities of their dogs, there is considerably less interest in field trials than in dog shows. In order for dogs to become full Champions, certain breeds must qualify in the field as well. Upon gaining three CCs in the show ring, the dog is designated a Show Champion (Sh Ch). The title Champion (Ch) requires that the dog gain an award at a field trial, be a 'special qualifier' at a field trial or pass a 'special show dog qualifier' judged by a field trial judge on a shooting day.

AGILITY TRIALS

Agility trials began in the United Kingdom in 1977 and have since spread around the world, especially to the United States, where they are very popular. The handler directs his dog over an obstacle course that includes jumps (such as those used in the working trials), as well as tyres, the dog walk, weave poles, pipe tunnels, collapsed tunnels, etc. The Kennel Club requires that dogs not be trained for agility until they are 12 months old. This dog sport is great fun for dog and owner and interested owners should join a training club that has obstacles and experienced

HOW TO ENTER A DOG SHOW

1. Obtain an entry form and show schedule from the Show Secretary.
2. Select the classes that you want to enter and complete the entry form.
3. Transfer your dog into your name at The Kennel Club. (Be sure that this matter is handled before entering.)
4. Find out how far in advance show entries must be made. Oftentimes it's more than a couple of months.

Breed judging at the 1999 Crufts Dog Show—the UK's best Pointers competing for the ticket.

agility handlers who can introduce you and your dog to the 'ropes' (and tyres, tunnels,etc.).

FÉDÉRATION CYNOLOGIQUE INTERNATIONALE

Established in 1911, the Fédération Cynologique Internationale (FCI) represents the 'world kennel club.' This international body brings uniformity to the breeding, judging and showing of purebred dogs. Although the FCI originally included only five European nations: France, Germany, Austria, the Netherlands and Belgium (which remains its headquarters), the organisation today embraces nations on six continents and recognises well over 300 breeds of purebred dog. There are three titles attainable through the FCI: the International Champion, which is the most prestigious; the International Beauty Champion, which is based on aptitude certificates in different countries; and the International Trial Champion, which is based on achievement in obedience trials in different countries. Dogs from every country can participate in these impressive canine spectacles, the largest of which is the World Dog Show, hosted in a different country each year. FCI sponsors both national and international shows. The hosting country determines the judging system and breed standards are always

PRACTISE AT HOME

If you have decided to show your dog, you must train him to gait around the ring by your side at the correct pace and pattern, and to tolerate being handled and examined by the judge. Most breeds require complete dentition, all require a particular bite (scissor, level or undershot), and all males must have two apparently normal testicles fully descended into the scrotum. Enlist family and friends to hold mock trials in your garden to prepare your future champion!

A first-place Pointer strikes a winning pose with his handler.

Besides the World Dog Show, you can exhibit your dog at speciality shows held by different breed clubs. Speciality shows may have their own regulations.

Junior handling is a wonderful opportunity for young people to get involved and gain experience in the world of dog showing.

based on the breed's country of origin.

The FCI is divided into ten 'Groups.' At the World Dog Show, the following 'Classes' are offered for each breed: Puppy Class (6–9 months), Youth Class (9–18 months), Open Class (15 months or older) and Champion Class. A dog can be awarded a classification of Excellent, Very Good, Good, Sufficient and Not Sufficient. Puppies can be awarded classifications of Very Promising, Promising or Not Promising. Four placements are made in each class. After all sexes and classes are judged, a Best of Breed is selected. Other special groups and classes may also be shown. Each exhibitor showing a dog receives a written evaluation from the judge.

INDEX

*Page numbers in **boldface** indicate illustrations.*

Moulton College Library Resources Centre

This book is due for return on or before the last date shown below.

Dog _____

Date _____ Photographer _____